# Complex Problems, Negotiated Solutions

## Tools to Reduce Conflict in Community Development

Michael Warner

ITDG
PUBLISHING

Published by ITDG Publishing
103–105 Southampton Row, London WC1B 4HL, UK
www.itdgpublishing.org.uk


© Overseas Development Institute 2001
Cover design: Sue Michniewicz

First published in 2001

ISBN 185339 532 3

A catalogue record for this book is available from the British Library.


ITDG Publishing is the publishing arm of the Intermediate Technology
Development Group. Our mission is to build the skills and capacity of
people in developing countries through the dissemination of information
in all forms, enabling them to improve the quality of their lives and that of
future generations.


The Overseas Development Institute is Britain's leading independent
think-tank on international development and humanitarian issues. Its
mission is to inspire and inform policy and practice which lead to the
reduction of poverty, the alleviation of suffering and the achievement of
sustainable livelihoods in developing countries. It does this by locking
together high-quality applied research, practical policy advice and policy-
focused dissemination and debate.

Edited and typeset by Paul Mundy, Bergisch Gladbach, Germany
Printed in Great Britain by SRP Limited, Exeter

# Contents

# Appendices

---

*Conflict management* is about building capacities to cope with a changing world. At the local level, it is about strengthening individuals, groups and institutions to be able to manage the stresses associated with social disputes, local economic grievances and hostilities in a way that reduces conflict as a **constraint** to sustainable rural livelihoods and, where practicable, turns it into a positive social force.

*Consensus building* is one strategy for managing conflict. In contrast to strategies based on avoidance, force or compromise, consensus building seeks to facilitate agreement between individuals, groups or institutions based on mutual gains. By slowly broadening people's understanding of their own and others' interests and needs, and encouraging them to think outside often entrenched and emotional positions, win–win outcomes become entirely plausible.

The role of consensus building in sustainable livelihoods is not limited to conflict management. It has a critical part to play in exploiting **opportunities** to protect and enhance social and human capital, and can provide the skills needed to renegotiate the ways in which external actors contribute to transforming livelihood assets into beneficial outcomes.

---

# Figures

# Tables

# Boxes

# Training Exercises

# Acknowledgements

The origins of this book lie in a programme of conflict management implemented across a range of community-based natural resource projects in the Fiji Islands and Papua New Guinea. This programme is managed by the United Kingdom Foundation for the Peoples of the South Pacific (UKFSP) through its South Pacific affiliates, with funding from the Conflict and Humanitarian Assistance Department of the Department for International Development (DFID).

The Overseas Development Institute (ODI) has been involved in preparing guidelines to facilitate the above programme, culminating in 'A Manual on Alternative Conflict Management for Community-Based Natural Resource Projects in the South Pacific: Context, Principles, Tools and Training Materials'. Significant contributions to this manual were made by Dr Philip Scott Jones of the Centre for Rural Development Training, University of Wolverhampton, and by field staff from the Foundation for the People of the South Pacific in Fiji (especially Roshni Chand and Koto Simion), the Foundation for People and Community Development in Papua New Guinea (especially Katherine Yuave), and the PEACE Foundation Melanesia (especially Pat Howley) in Papua New Guinea.

This book builds on the earlier version. It has been re-orientated to address the emerging concept of sustainable rural livelihoods (see Introduction). The approach assumes that the principles and tools of conflict management and consensus building can contribute to achieving sustainable rural livelihoods. The book draws on a wide range of field experiences and on published and unpublished materials, listed in the References. The three most utilized sources are a course handbook on facilitation by Hickling and Acland (1994), a resource pack for conflict transformation from International Alert (Doucet, 1996), and a paper by Warner and Jones (1998).

Special thanks to: Andrew Acland and Allen Hickling for an inspirational training workshop in 1998 which set these ideas in motion; Dr John Farrington and all at the Overseas Development Institute, London; Dr Paul Mundy, who took on the not insignificant burden of editing and readying the manuscript for publication; and all at ITDG Publishing, London.

The author would like to thank IIED for permission to adapt material from Warner et al. (1996) in writing Chapter 9. We have been unable to trace the copyright holder of Appendix 1 and would welcome any information enabling us to do so.

# Chapter 1

# Introduction

## Who is this book for?

This book is intended for people who have to deal with, and find solutions to, conflicts in rural areas of developing countries. It will be especially useful for staff of international and national non-governmental organizations (NGOs), advisers in donor agencies working on rural livelihoods, government departments and private companies.

The book is designed to be relevant to most types of rural livelihood projects and interventions. These include:

o   Projects managed by community groups, for example in participatory forestry, community-based coastal resource management, integrated conservation and development, community water supply and sanitation infrastructure, and community-based revolving credit.

o   Interventions where community-owned resources and capital are managed by outside organizations, such as logging firms, medium-scale mining companies, commercial agriculture enterprises, water and electricity utilities, tourism operators, microfinance NGOs and commercial community-based organizations.

## Participation and sustainable livelihoods

This book promotes public involvement in sustainable development. It offers practical guidance on how conflict management and consensus building can help achieve sustainable rural livelihoods.

The past 15 years have seen increasing interest in community participation as a way to make development projects more sustainable. Negotiation is an important mechanism for such participation. This book provides guidance on how to establish and manage a process of negotiation that involves the various stakeholders in rural development.

The methods described in this book fit well within the 'sustainable rural livelihoods' framework espoused by DFID and other donor agencies. The livelihoods framework involves five main elements (Figure 1.1):

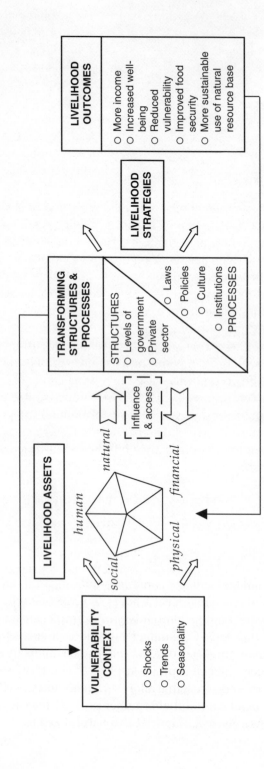

**Figure 1.1** Sustainable livelihoods framework (source: Carney, 1999)

2

- o **Livelihood assets** The different forms of capital – financial, social, human, natural and physical – that rural people may (or may not) have, and their ability to put these to use.
- o **Vulnerability context** The impact of external events and trends (economic, natural environment, population growth, technological change, violence) and seasonality on livelihoods.
- o **Transforming structures and processes** The institutions and organizations (government, private sector, etc.) and processes (policies, institutions, law, etc.) that affect the way people use the livelihood assets.
- o **Livelihood strategies** The various ways that rural people make a living: farming, fishing, trade, wage labour, migration, etc.
- o **Livelihood outcomes** The results of these strategies: income, well-being, security, sustainable resource use, etc.

Conflict management and consensus building can affect these elements by exploiting the opportunities and reducing the constraints they embody. They can exploit opportunities by:
- o protecting and building all five types of capital assets – particularly social and human
- o renegotiating the role of government and private organizations, so enabling the livelihood assets to be transformed into benefits.

They can reduce the constraints in the livelihood framework elements by:
- o managing disputes within civil society, and between civil society and external actors
- o helping to prevent violent conflict, and enabling people to cope with and recover from violence.

These approaches are discussed below in the context of managing conflicts.


## Building and protecting capital assets

In themselves, conflict-management and consensus-building skills are a form of human capital. Skills that enable local leaders to negotiate with public water authorities or private logging companies, for example, are empowering in their own right. .But conflict-management and consensus-building skills provide far more than this. They offer a rapid and cost-effective means of protecting and enhancing social capital – aspects of social organization such as the networks, norms and trust that allow society to function (Putman, 1993). It is human and social capital that together provide the capacity for protecting and enhancing physical, financial and natural assets.

For example, productive common property resources (forests, rivers, etc.) require robust social organizations, and people need skills for such organizations to emerge. People need also to negotiate with the formal or informal authorities, develop rules to govern competition over resources and manage those resources, and ensure access to alternative income sources for those excluded. Roads (physical capital) and credit (financial capital) will remain inaccessible if people lack the capacity to negotiate access to transportation services or to affordable repayment terms.

Consensus building can play a particular role in protecting and enhancing social and human capital. Jealousies, tensions, disputes and violence can undermine co-ordination and co-operation both among local people and between local groups and outsiders. Conflict-management skills can help prevent this.

Table 1.1 shows some of the ways consensus building can contribute to building different types of social and human capital.

Table 1.1. Role of consensus building in strengthening the social and human capital component of livelihoods: examples from Fiji and Papua New Guinea

| Form of social/human capital | Examples |
|---|---|
| Family and kinship connections | Mediation by a local NGO in family disputes such as domestic violence, drunkenness and attempted rape |
| Horizontal social networks, associations, networks of civic engagement | Training of village chiefs and Mataqali (landowner) heads in facilitating consensus among stakeholders over harvesting forest resources, profit distribution and project membership |
| | NGO brokering multiple land claims in a conservation and livelihood project. Disputing parties agreed to proportional access to future revenue streams (e.g. logging, oil palm, tourists) rather than delineating land-ownership boundaries |
| Horizontal trust, norms and rules independent of linkages between civil society organizations | Third-party facilitation by an NGO in the above project over the distribution of tourist revenues. Agreement was based on separating responsibilities for different service activities; the parties accepted mutually beneficial arrangements for engaging with tourists. In a community forestry project, disenfranchised groups (e.g. those without forest resources) were given more say in formulating rules for resource access (they received income for allowing their land to be crossed) and in project participation (they could become involved in wood-processing and marketing) |

Source: ODI (1998)

## Renegotiating the role of external actors

Not all rural people are farmers, and many farmers earn a large part of their livelihood from activities other than agriculture. The livelihood framework recognizes this. It separates the link between 'rural' and 'agriculture', and widens the scope for rural development to other sectors – health, education, training, infrastructure, financial services, etc. This calls for new associations between external structures (ministries, local authorities, firms, other stakeholders) and processes (policies, laws, cultures) on one hand, and the intended project beneficiaries on the other.

Such 'vertical' associations may be a prerequisite to strong local, 'horizontal' associations, in that they facilitate effective local representation, participation and institutional accountability (Harriss and de Renzio, 1997). However, emerging evidence (e.g. McIntosh et al., 2000) suggests that the importance of external social capital in strengthening civil society may be overstated.

This is because many disputes, and even some violent conflicts, are underpinned as much by localized competition over power, resource distribution and access to limited economic opportunities, as by structural injustices. The continuing violence in South Africa could, for example, be attributed in part to the replacement of political injustice of a structural nature with highly visible local economic inequalities.

This means it is not always necessary to address structural injustices in order to strengthen civil society and build social and other assets. Consensus building can find creative and lateral solutions to problems in the short to medium term, build co-operation and co-ordination, and reduce tensions – without the assistance of government institutions, and without having to resolve the structural, root causes of the conflict. Table 1.1 gives some examples of this.

In addition, consensus building can contribute to stronger co-ordination and co-operation between civil society and external institutions – central and local government, firms and statutory institutions – helping transform livelihood assets into sustainable benefits (Table 1.2).

## Managing contested processes of participation

A 'livelihoods' approach enables planners to identify possible interventions with the aim of reducing rural poverty. But attempts to improve the economic security of the poor may well increase tensions, especially with groups that are excluded from immediate benefits – for example, entrepreneurs who own the vehicles needed to transport produce.

The concept of civil society as a 'contested space' runs counter to the earlier notion of civil society as a single entity, with the different organizations

5

**Table 1.2. Use of consensus building in renegotiating the role of external institutions in rural livelihoods: examples from Fiji and Papua New Guinea**

| Form of social capital | Examples |
| --- | --- |
| Cross-sectoral (vertical) linkages, e.g. partnerships between private sector, government agencies and civil society | Training community-based and non-governmental organizations to negotiate with private companies:<br><br>O Removing the threat of large-scale clear felling by an oil palm firm in a parks-and-people project<br>O Replacing landowner roadblocks with revenue-sharing arrangements between logging firms and local landowners<br>O Agreeing profit distribution and tourist trail routes between community leaders and tour operators.<br><br>Third-party facilitation to formulate rules for participation in a project. For example, drawing up a memorandum of understanding in a coral aquaculture project (detailing the expected benefits for and responsibilities of each party), and individual agreements between participating households and the project sponsor. |
| Macro-level social capital (constitutions, regulations, laws, statutory institutions and policies) | Strengthening of formal institutional processes of conflict management to mediate disputes. For example, training local land mediators, village magistrates and officers from the government Lands Department to resolve disputes over land ownership Training in consensual negotiation and mediation skills for staff from the Department of Environment and Lands Department to reduce delays in the approval of infrastructure projects, and bring the process of land-claim arbitration closer to the local level. |

Source: ODI (1998)

working towards common objectives of democratic governance. McIlwaine (1998, p. 656) forcibly puts this point in the context of El Salvador. Her argument is that: 'civil society and the social relations that underpin it are not, by their nature, inherently democratic or participatory. Nor does strengthening civil society organizations automatically engender democratization. Indeed, it may actually undermine it.'

Conflict management offers a set of principles and tools for managing the evolution of civil society organizations and groups, and for defusing conflict among them. In particular, they can be be used to strengthen the existing customary and quasi-legal mechanisms for resolving disputes. Box 1.1 gives an example where conflict management transformed a dispute between two community organizations into a force promoting more sustainable rural livelihoods.

Conflict management can equip natural resource projects, such as community forestry and mariculture, to manage tensions as and when they arise.

## Box 1.1. Managing a conflict over a tourist guesthouse (Papua New Guinea)

### The conflict

In 1997, with financial and technical help from the Foundation for People and Community Development (FPCD), community groups in the Kakoro region of the proposed Lakekamu Basin Conservation Area constructed a tourist guesthouse. As tourists and scientists began to arrive, a dispute broke out between two local women's groups over how to distribute profits from the guesthouse cooking and cleaning services. The tourist influx soon ceased, along with the flow of income. FPCD considered withdrawing from the project, and an evaluation cited the dispute as evidence that the Lakekamu initiative – of which the guesthouse was a part – was unlikely to be cost-effective.

### The conflict-management process

Using simple office-based analytical tools, FPCD staff mapped out the causes of the dispute, the stakeholders involved, their immediate concerns and underlying motivations. The information was then verified with the stakeholders. This month-long process also built the degree of trust needed for FPCD to act as a facilitator. After a series of separate focus group discussions, a joint meeting was held at which a settlement was negotiated. The meeting format was designed to be familiar to the participants in terms of its location, eligibility to contribute, style of dialogue and type of decision making.

### The settlement

The process created awareness of the participants' own and each other's underlying motivations, focused discussion on common interests and solicited fresh ideas. It revealed that both sides shared a strong desire to see the dispute resolved, so tourists would return and income would once again flow to individuals and the community. It also became clear that the parties' true motivations had less to do with profits from the guesthouse per se, and more with being involved in some way in earning income from the tourists. Through free and open discussion, and with FPCD clarifying the economic and technical viability of the various ideas, it was agreed that one of the groups (the Community Women's Group) would voluntarily leave the guesthouse services to the other (the Guest House Women's Group). In return, the former group would provide porter services for the guesthouse, and would make and sell handicrafts. This group would also assume responsibility for collecting and selling kunai grasses to help construct housing for FPCD staff, and develop a small kerosene-trading business from earlier guesthouse profits. Finally, the group was granted sole responsibility for providing cooking and cleaning services to the staff housing once this was completed. The overall settlement was tested for its social acceptability with the men and community leaders. Six weeks later, the settlement appears to be holding.

7

It can do this by integrating into project design the management of existing, and the prevention of anticipated, disputes. It can combine this with building the capacity of project intermediaries in negotiation and third-party facilitation (ICIMOD, 1996; Resolve, 1994).

## Preventing, coping with and recovering from violent conflict

At any one time, there may be 20 high-intensity conflicts (wars with more than 1000 deaths) (e.g. Algeria, Bosnia, the African Great Lakes) and over 100 lower-intensity conflicts with fewer deaths (e.g. Sri Lanka, northern Uganda, eastern Turkey). Many of these latter conflicts are long term, subsiding and escalating over time so that sporadic violence and the threat of violence become the accepted social norm. While at the beginning of the twentieth century, 90 per cent of war casualties were military, nowadays over 95 per cent are civilian. As well as death and injury, the civilian impacts of conflict include displacement, hunger and disease.

Sustaining livelihoods in conflict-prone areas requires capabilities to cope with the threat and reality of violence, and to contribute to recovery and post-conflict reconstruction. Conflict-management and consensus-building skills can play a part in this (Ndelu, 1998). However, this book is not designed for situations of open, armed conflict (for this, see Doucet, 1996).

The principles and tools discussed in this book are more applicable to situations of post-conflict reconstruction – especially where this involves civil society and local capacities – and to preventing latent conflicts from turning violent.

In addition to violent conflict, many other countries and regions are in a state of latent conflict. Armed conflicts may be subsiding or re-emerging. Or various structural injustices (land ownership, access to the media, etc.) or local economic grievances (such as competition over limited income-earning opportunities) are raising tensions to levels that present a risk of violence.

Latent conflict can also exist in a regional context. For example, relatively stable countries are threatened by violence in neighbouring countries, and economically significant but overexploited natural resources (such as rivers) cross national borders.

Projects in areas of latent conflict sometimes provoke or awaken disputes. In turn, these disputes sometimes feed on existing political or economic tensions, and can escalate into hostilities and violence. The social or political environment may be damaged without the project itself being undermined. But all too often, the project itself can be harmed through threats to staff, delays in activities, office relocations, adverse media coverage, loss of access to beneficiaries and unforeseen costs.

A number of rural development projects funded by DFID have incorporated conflict-management and consensus-building principles to reduce the damage caused by conflicts, and to help prevent conflicts and build peace. One aim has been to use conflict management tools to reduce tensions and economic grievances *in situ*, thereby removing one of the key factors pushing rural people towards the towns, where a mixing of cultural groups and poverty may trigger violence. Table 1.3 lists some ways conflict management and consensus building can reduce livelihood vulnerabilities and exploit opportunities for building peace.

# Project cycle management

The approaches described in this book can be used at different stages in the project cycle: to manage conflicts that occur during the project implementation and to avoid potential conflicts identified while a project is being planned.

## Managing conflicts during project implementation

The first strategy is to manage disputes and conflicts that arise while a project is being implemented. This may involve resolving the conflict altogether, i.e. not only managing the immediate cause of the dispute, but also removing all underlying contributing factors. Because these factors are often structural and operate at the national or regional level (e.g. land-tenure legislation, economic policy, political expediency, etc.), it may not be possible to resolve the conflict completely. In such instances, the conflict must be 'managed' rather than resolved:

o   to prevent existing conflicts from escalating;
o   to prevent latent conflicts from re-emerging;
o   where possible, to transform the conflict into a force for positive social change; and
o   to manage structural conflicts such that they no longer interfere with the efficient implementation of the project or intervention.

This emphasis on management rather than resolution is what underpins the term 'conflict management'. The task of true conflict resolution may be best left to other areas of development and peace building: policy reform, structural adjustment, institutional capacity building, democratization, and

**Table 1.3.** The role of conflict management and consensus building in reducing livelihood vulnerability and exploiting opportunities in conflict-prone areas

| | Type of conflict situation | | | |
|---|---|---|---|---|
| | Latent conflict/submerged tensions | Threat of violence/rising tensions | Open conflict/violent conflict | Fragile periods/post-conflict rehabilitation & reconstruction |
| **Political processes and structures** | ○ Promote legitimate representative authorities<br>○ Promote participatory development<br>○ Promote competency, transparency and accountability in public institutions & local organizations<br>○ Advocacy | ○ Promote conflict resolution 'entrepreneurs' and advocates<br>○ Support legitimate representative authorities<br>○ Contribute to community-based mediation efforts<br>○ Support mediation efforts between warring parties | ○ Contribute to maintaining lines of communication between protagonists & civil population<br>○ Capitalize on windows of opportunity for peace building<br>○ Facilitate co-ordination between security, diplomacy, humanitarian aid & development organizations<br>○ Contribute to re-establishment of rule of law | ○ Strengthen legitimate representative authority<br>○ Contribute to legitimate political re-integration<br>○ Catalyse discussion of unresolved structural roots of conflict<br>○ Facilitate government endorsement of local peace-building efforts |
| **Economic trends, structures, activities and processes** | ○ Improve access to and management of natural resources for poor & disadvantaged<br>○ Promote economic balance & fair competition among civil society organizations | ○ Design low-profile interventions & avoid conspicuous assets | | ○ Focus on meeting immediate needs but with a view towards development objectives<br>○ Contribute economic incentives to the mainstreaming of settlements<br>○ Promote immediate and visible economic benefits<br>○ Rehabilitate financial institutions |

*(continued)*

Table 1.3 (continued)

| | Type of conflict situation | | | |
|---|---|---|---|---|
| | Latent conflict/submerged tensions | Threat of violence/rising tensions | Open conflict/violent conflict | Fragile periods/post-conflict rehabilitation & reconstruction |
| **Social processes, institutions, behaviour, values and relationships** | o Promote accountable, effective, formal law & order<br>o Support capacity building to promote adaptability to rising tensions & social change<br>o Build and strengthen social networks, both horizontal and vertical<br>o Build capacity for civil society to manage its own internal competitive tendencies<br>o Provide facilitation & dispute-resolution services | o Create 'safe spaces' for non-confrontational & non-political dialogue<br>o Promote communications between potentially conflicting parties<br>o Promote shared understanding of each party's underlying fears & motivations<br>o Promote self-help & self-management in crisis-threatened populations<br>o Promote awareness about conflict, its causes, impacts, prevention & escalation<br>o Promote networks of conciliation services<br>o Strengthen troubleshooting & negotiation capabilities of civil society<br>o Promote a culture of dispute resolution & conflict management within civil society | o Contribute to 'second-tracking' mediation processes | o Contribute to reconciliation processes<br>o Build local constituencies for peace<br>o Strengthen conflict management mechanisms proven as effective<br>o Promote mechanisms to defuse violence or tensions<br>o Provide incentives which contribute to effectiveness of settlements |

Compiled from Lederach (1994), Bush (1998), DFID (1997), O'Reilly (1998), Goodhand and Hulme (1997) and OECD (1998)

international conventions and protocols. However, where a project can contribute to these wider peace-building processes, such opportunities should be exploited.

## Improving project planning

The second strategy is to build conflict-prevention measures into the design of projects before they are implemented. This approach is analogous to environmental impact assessment, where effects (in this case, conflicts) are first predicted and the project design is then revised to mitigate the most significant threats.

## The structure of the book

The remainder of this book is divided into 14 chapters. Chapter 2 places the process of consensus building within the context of the different strategies for managing conflict. Chapters 3 and 4 describe the core principles of consensus building. Chapter 5 introduces the process of consensus building.

Chapters 6 to 10 give details of the various stages of consensus building, and present a series of tools that can be used at each stage. These chapters follow the same order as the consensus building process, though as the text stresses, this order is not fixed and steps may occur simultaneously or be repeated as required.

Chapter 6 describes how to undertake an initial office-based conflict analysis. Chapter 7 discusses a provisional conflict-management plan, while Chapter 8 outlines how to undertake participatory conflict analysis. Chapter 9 focuses on the conflict analysis framework – an approach that is particularly useful in dealing with complex conflicts. Chapter 10 focuses briefly on capacity building for stakeholders, while Chapter 11 describes the negotiations that aim to lead to consensus.

Chapters 12 to 15 outline some additional tools useful in consensual negotiation and other stages in the conflict-management process. Chapter 12 describes the functions and ethics of facilitation. Chapter 13 outlines the design and methodology of holding workshops for consensual negotiation and training to build capacity. Chapter 14 gives some ideas on how to manage difficult people, while Chapter 15 outlines some tools useful in consensual negotiation.

# How to use this book

This book can be used in different ways:

- As a training manual for use in a course on consensual negotiation. It contains numerous exercises that the trainer can use with a class. The course participants may be students, agency staff or stakeholders in a rural development project. The Appendices contain background information for several of the role-playing exercises. They can be photocopied and given to the participants. The book was originally designed for a course lasting 10 days but, depending on the type of participants and their needs, shorter courses could be compiled. For example, Chapters 12–15 have been used as the basis of a three-day course on third-party facilitation for staff of NGOs and donors in the UK.
- As a self-learning manual. The case studies and exercises will be particularly useful for this purpose.
- As reference materials. The approaches and tools described can be used in a variety of ways to manage conflicts, as well as in other situations.

# Chapter 2

# Conflict management

## What is conflict?

'Conflict is a very fluid, mobile, ambiguous word. In different contexts, it can mean different things to different people. For example, it can refer to:

o    a debate or contest;
o    a disagreement, argument, dispute, quarrel;
o    a struggle, battle or confrontation; or
o    a state of unrest, turmoil or chaos.

All of these can be used to characterise situations in different social settings – from the inner emotional or psychological process of the individual, to relationships within or between different social groups (such as the family, town, states, cultures or even civilisation).

The word conflict usually has negative connotations. We tend to think of it as the opposite of co-operation, harmony, accord, or even peace. Within everyday usage it is most closely associated with, and often used to mean, the same as violence. It is not surprising then that most people think of conflict as destructive and undesirable, as a social aberration to be avoided, contained or eliminated… Such a narrow and one-dimensional account of conflict is unhelpful, because it does not allow us to distinguish between different levels of conflict or the various forms it may take or the many causes involved in conflict-behaviour, and it does not help us to think clearly through the most appropriate responses' (Doucet, 1996, vol. 2, p. 3).

Conflict should be seen as an expression of a changing society. Nowhere, perhaps, are societies changing more rapidly than in certain rural areas of developing countries. New technologies, commercialization of common property resources, privatization of public services, growing consumerism and government policies for managing natural resources – all are pressing individuals and communities to adapt. Conflict is therefore not something that can be avoided or suppressed. It needs to be acknowledged, managed and transformed into a force for positive social change.

---

### Box 2.1. Conflicts in society

Conflicts can occur at all levels in society:
o  Within an individual
o  Between husband and wife
o  Within a household
o  Between extended family groups
o  Among community groups (councils, associations, co-operatives, land-owners, resource users, etc.)
o  Between community groups and external organizations (NGOs, government agencies and commercial companies)
o  Between different ethnic groups
o  Between political parties
o  Between countries and groups of countries.

---

# Conflict and rural livelihood projects

Conflicts may arise within many different types of rural development projects. Such projects fall into three broad categories: (a) where local people both own and manage the resources; (b) where they own the resources but do not manage them directly; and (c) where they manage resources owned by others.

*Where local people or community groups own and manage the resources*  Such projects may cover:
o    smallholder agriculture;
o    ecoforestry, e.g. involving portable sawmills, community forest management and timber processing of indigenous forests or plantations;

15

o  coastal resource management: the management of fish stocks, coral extraction, aquaculture, etc., by community groups;
o  integrated conservation and development projects, with community
   groups providing research and tourism accommodation, guides, crafts
   and other services, often in co-ordination with tour operators;
o  other ecotourism projects;
o  community-based wildlife management;
o  community-based credit schemes.

*Where local people or community groups own the resources but are not
involved in direct management*   In this case, the resources are managed by
outsiders – other community groups, public bodies or private organizations.
Local people benefit from the employment or revenue the project generates.
Such projects may include:
o  logging and timber processing;
o  some agriculture projects;
o  commercial silviculture;
o  small- and medium-scale extractive industries.

*Where local people or community groups manage resources owned by
others*   In this case, the assets may be owned by other community groups,
public bodies or private organizations. Many livelihood projects that aim to
reduce poverty fall into this category.

   Livelihood projects may be started by an outside agency (government or
non-governmental), or by people in the community itself. This book is relevant to both types of project.
   Conflicts may have various negative effects. They may lower the overall effectiveness and sustainability of the project. They may cause the
project to collapse completely, destroying local participation and causing the outside assistance to be withdrawn. They may even escalate into
physical violence.
   Box 2.2 outlines some of the disputes and conflicts common to different
types of livelihood projects.


## Types of conflict

Conflicts can be divided into two main types: those caused directly by the
introduction of new developmental (or environmental) pressures, and
dormant structural injustices that are reawakened by new development
pressures.

## Box 2.2. Common conflicts and disputes affecting livelihood projects

### Land disputes

o Disputes over land ownership of project sites
o Disputes over land boundaries between different land-owning groups
o Land-ownership disputes ignited by speculation by firms
o Disputes over access rights
o Disputes over renewal arrangements for leased land

### Income disputes

o Unfulfilled hopes for higher incomes
o Disputes over the distribution of employment and income from enterprises
o Jealousy due to growing wealth disparities

### Cultural and relationship conflicts

o Lack of co-operation between different community groups
o Cultural conflicts between community groups and outsiders
o Disputes over project management between community groups and outsiders
o Political interference (national, provincial or local)
o Latent family and relationship disputes
o Different expectations of community groups (e.g. landowners) and outsiders (e.g. firms)

### Resource-related disputes

o Competition for natural resources (e.g. wildlife, fish stocks, timber, other forest products) resulting from new technologies (e.g. motor vehicles, guns, sawmills, fishing nets)
o Environmental damage by one group of resource users affecting another group
o Unplanned exploitation of resources opened up by the project's access roads
o Some landowners (e.g. those near the road) benefit more than others

## Developmental pressures

Conflicts over natural resources are often blamed on a combination of demographic changes and the limited sustainability of renewable natural resources. For example, rising populations may overwhelm traditional grazing areas, or migrants from the lowlands may compete for land with upland farmers. However, conflicts are rarely as simple as this. A wide range of developmental pressures confronts rural communities:

o New productivity-enhancing technologies (e.g. artificial fertilizers, agricultural mechanization, permanent irrigation, joint management regimes). If poorly managed, these can damage the ability of a natural resource to regenerate.

o Growing awareness among rural people that common property (land, minerals, forests, fish and wildlife) can have commercial value. Some realize that they can benefit if they claim private property rights. Elites are often able to capture these benefits for themselves.

o Increasing importance of the cash economy to rural people and rising aspirations for consumer products.

o Lack of incentive for community groups and outsiders to avoid harming the environment or other people.

o Declining government expenditure on services such as health, education, water, electricity and transportation in rural areas.

o New conservation policies, e.g. laws to protect wildlife.

o New government policies giving communities responsibility to manage state-owned resources.

o Migration to the cities, reducing the labour available to manage rural resources.

o Employment changes arising from new rural-based industries, e.g. crop processing, manufacturing, extractive industries, oil and gas, and construction.

Poor enforcement of regulations is a frequent cause of conflicts:

o Regulatory agencies often lack resources to enforce environmental protection regulations contained in licenses, permits, etc.

o Large companies avoid compliance and sanctions by threatening to withdraw their investment or by manipulating the system, including the courts.

o Industries, governmental agencies and the general population generally do not understand environmental laws and regulations.

o Pollution-control requirements are unrealistic, and plans to mitigate environmental impacts are poorly implemented, leading to non-compliance.

o The courts fail to enforce regulations because of prolonged legal processes. One or more parties may not support the outcome of court cases.

Even if a community is not subject to these pressures now, it may well be in the future.


## Structural conflicts

The link between common developmental pressures and degradation of natural resources is well documented. But these pressures may be only part of the cause of the degradation. They are often underpinned by deeper, structural conflicts: inequalities in legal definitions of land ownership, local and regional economic and political differences, and ethnic and cultural differences.

Many of these factors lie dormant until reawakened by a particular set of developmental pressures. The following is an example:

> A dispute over a land title arises between community groups due to a combination of two factors: the rising number of young men who need landholdings (demographic change) and the emergence of a new market for forest products from an area of communal land previously used only for subsistence (a new development pressure). For six months, the two principal community groups compete over the forest resources, both extracting at unsustainable rates. After six months, one group decides to turn to the legal system to solve the dispute. This reawakens what had not been a significant problem – the ambiguous land tenure system. The system – a remnant of colonial days – takes no account of the strength of historic claims to land. The court grants legal ownership of a large portion of the forest to one of the groups. In response, the other group concentrates its activities within the remaining area of communal land, degrading it even faster. At the same time, other community groups are prevented from using the land.

Figure 2.1 illustrates the events in this example. Table 2.1 lists some structural conflicts relevant to sustainable rural livelihoods and which, when reawakened, can contribute to more rapid degradation of natural resources.

In general, then, unsustainable management of a resource may be only partly related to the finite nature of the resource, or to new and unmanageable commercial pressures. It may have just as much to do with reawakened structural inequalities and ethnic differences. Conflicts over resources are enmeshed in a complex web of sensitive natural environments, new developmental pressures, structural economic and legal inequalities, personal and ethnic differences, and the interests of individuals, groups and organizations from both inside and outside rural communities. This complexity has caused conventional, adversarial forms of conflict resolution to fail. This in turn has generated interest in the practices of consensual negotiation.

19

**Table 2.1.  Types of structural conflicts relevant to rural livelihoods**

| Type | Key characteristics | Examples |
|---|---|---|
| **Social** | Unequal, unjust or unrepresentative social structures | O Different levels of education or income: some parties are less able to negotiate or use legal channels<br>O Insecure land leases: natural resources are exploited rather than harvested |
| **Legal** | Legal systems with bias towards certain stakeholders | O Legal systems that recognize only 'named' landowners and not all resource users. |
| **Economic** | Economic or political power biased towards certain stakeholders | O Economic and political power of commercial companies<br>O Government policies and permit arrangements for extractive industries ignore customary ownership norms |
| **Cultural** | Groups hold deep-seated values that define their identity | O Indigenous people and migrants hold different values for land<br>O Elites and politicians exploit racial, religious, tribal, ethnic or linguistic differences and prejudices<br>O Groups dislike each other |

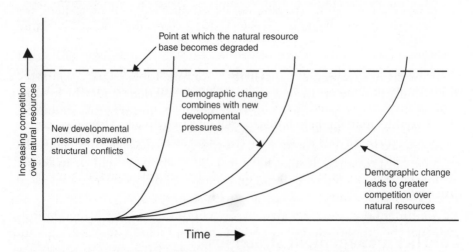

**Figure 2.1.** Contribution of demographic change, developmental pressures and structural conflicts to resource degradation

20

## Conflict escalation

Conflicts are best thought of as dynamic, interactive, social-cum-political processes rather than single, self-contained events. No two conflicts are identical, but the ways they emerge and subside (i.e. move from stability to instability, and back again) are often similar. At any time, a conflict may be at one of a number of stages of transformation. It moves from stage to stage, not always in the same direction, but backwards and forwards, sometimes stagnating at one point for a considerable period.

Figure 2.2 shows the stages of conflict escalation and some of the key characteristics of each. Conflicts at each stage are managed in different ways. Strategies to manage disputes or non-violent confrontation will aim to prevent an escalation towards violence. As conflicts become more confrontational, conflict management tends to split into two distinct strategies. One is to try to reduce further escalation. The other is to prepare to mitigate the effects if violence does occur. Figure 2.3 shows some of the ways the conflicting parties, governments, NGOs and donors can manage conflicts at different stages.

## Conflict management strategies

There is no perfect process for managing the vulnerability of livelihoods. The overall strategy adopted in each project should be the most practicable one, taking into account the available resources, the capabilities of the people

21

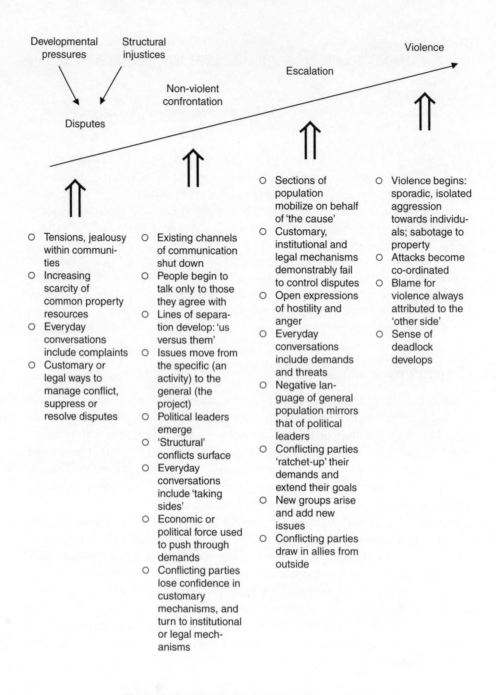

**Developmental pressures**  **Structural injustices**

**Violence**

**Escalation**

**Non-violent confrontation**

**Disputes**

○ Tensions, jealousy within communities
○ Increasing scarcity of common property resources
○ Everyday conversations include complaints
○ Customary or legal ways to manage conflict, suppress or resolve disputes

○ Existing channels of communication shut down
○ People begin to talk only to those they agree with
○ Lines of separation develop: 'us versus them'
○ Issues move from the specific (an activity) to the general (the project)
○ Political leaders emerge
○ 'Structural' conflicts surface
○ Everyday conversations include 'taking sides'
○ Economic or political force used to push through demands
○ Conflicting parties lose confidence in customary mechanisms, and turn to institutional or legal mechanisms

○ Sections of population mobilize on behalf of 'the cause'
○ Customary, institutional and legal mechanisms demonstrably fail to control disputes
○ Open expressions of hostility and anger
○ Everyday conversations include demands and threats
○ Negative language of general population mirrors that of political leaders
○ Conflicting parties 'ratchet-up' their demands and extend their goals
○ New groups arise and add new issues
○ Conflicting parties draw in allies from outside

○ Violence begins: sporadic, isolated aggression towards individuals; sabotage to property
○ Attacks become co-ordinated
○ Blame for violence always attributed to the 'other side'
○ Sense of deadlock develops

**Figure 2.2.** Characteristics of conflict escalation

22

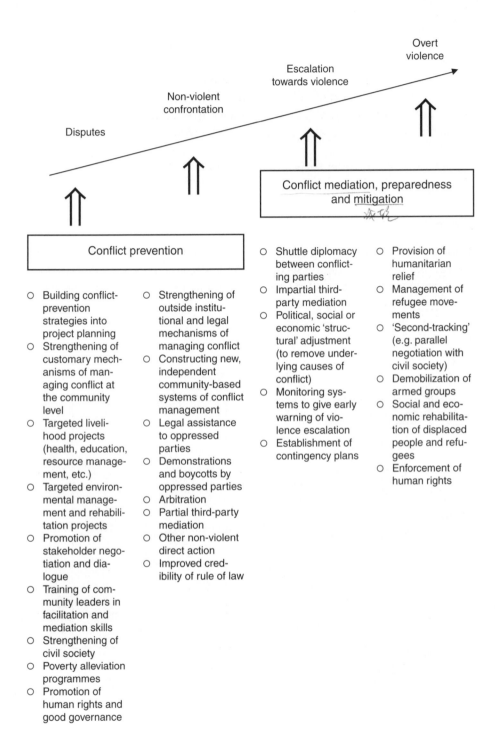

**Figure 2.3.** Conflict management options

or organizations involved, safety issues and the viable risk-management options.

Figure 2.4 summarizes five different strategies open to a conflicting party. The approaches differ depending on the value the party places on:

o   maintaining good relations with other parties; and

o   achieving its own goals.

Each of the five strategies is discussed briefly below.

## Force

Conflict is managed through force, where one party has the will and means to win regardless of whether its opponent loses, and irrespective of damage to its relationships. Not all parties are able to use force. Its use depends largely on the power that one party holds relative to another.

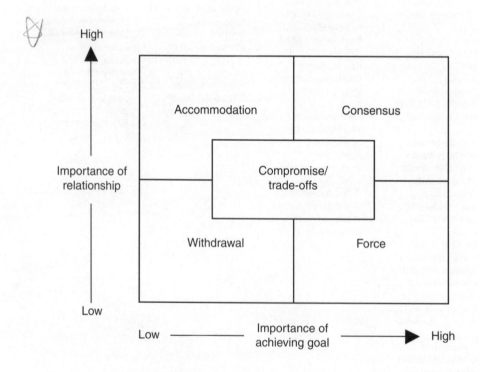

**Figure 2.4.**   Conflict management strategies (source: unknown)

Some of the more obvious uses of force include:

o   physical violence (actual or threatened);
o   exertion of economic dominance, e.g. buying out opponents;
o   corruption of government officials;
o   blackmail.

In some cases, recourse to the legal system is also a form of force, in that one party can use its superior resources to buy better advice or raise the stakes (for example, by appealing a lost case).

Some less obvious, but often no less powerful, forms of force include:

o   adversarial, uncompromising negotiation tactics;
o   political expediency;
o   manipulation of the electoral system;
o   use of the mass media to rally public support;
o   public protest;
o   witch hunts;
o   slander; and
o   threat of withdrawal.

## Withdrawal

Withdrawal is suited to those parties whose desire to avoid confrontation outweighs the goals they are trying to achieve. The power of withdrawal should not be underestimated, not least because the threat of withdrawal can persuade reluctant and sometimes more powerful parties to negotiate towards consensus. Types of withdrawal include:

o   avoidance;
o   opting out of a project or negotiations;
o   delaying tactics;
o   postponing a decision;
o   temporary boycott; and
o   strikes.

## Accommodation

Sometimes one party values a strong and continuing relationship with another party more highly than its own specific goals. In these cases, a party may choose to accommodate the other parties' goals, conceding to all or most of their demands. It may seem to have given in to force, but it thinks it has gained by securing good relations, perhaps some goodwill, and the option to achieve some greater goal in the future.

## Compromise

'Compromise' is often confused with 'consensus'. To compromise in a negotiation may sound positive, but it means that at least one of the parties
perceives that it has had to forgo something. In project planning, the no-
tions of 'compromise' and 'trade-offs' are now prevalent, spurred on by the
fear of the 'tragedy of the commons' and the need to allocate resources in a
rational way. For example, stakeholder analysis – an analytical tool often
used in designing community projects – requires planners to analyse how a
project will affect the various stakeholder groups. The process identifies
where the objectives of the different stakeholders conflict and where they
are in harmony. From this, an optimal trade-off with the minimum 'win–
lose' outcome can be designed.

In rural areas, many of the objectives of different stakeholders appear to
conflict. For example, poorer people may graze their cattle on land that
wealthier groups want to exploit commercially. Thus it is not uncommon
for people settling a dispute to make sacrifices and forgo opportunities. The
project must then be redesigned to promote this minimum 'win–lose' sce-
nario. This may include a bias towards maximizing benefits for the poor
and disenfranchized, but recognizes the political limitations of restricting
more powerful stakeholders.

## Consensus

Although consensus building sometimes includes elements of compromise
in the final agreement, there are some key differences between the two approaches. For example, consensus building explicitly sets out to avoid trade-
offs altogether, seeking to achieve a 'win–win' outcome. In contrast, a compromise approach seeks to minimize what are considered to be inevitable
trade-offs. Figure 2.5 illustrates these differences.

### Limitations of compromise
When planning livelihood projects to prevent conflict, and in resolving conflicts during project implementation, a compromise approach is limited by
a number of factors:
o   Stakeholder groups are identified narrowly, in relation to project bene-
    fits rather than conflict management.
o   Stakeholders' objectives are seen as 'fixed'.
o   Objectives for resource use are often generalized. This leads to the spatial,
    temporal and quantitative nature of potential conflicts being overstated.
o   The strategic components of the project design are seen as fixed, con-
    straining the search for mutually beneficial solutions.

26

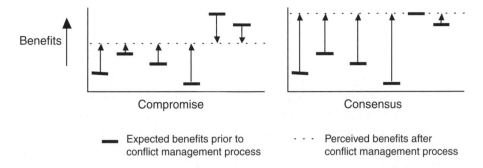

Benefits

Compromise        Consensus

— Expected benefits prior to    · · · Perceived benefits after
      conflict management process        conflict management process

**Figure 2.5.** Compromise vs. consensus approach to conflict management

o   Analysis, not negotiation, is emphasized. This limits the possibilities for creative and imaginative solutions.
o   Intangible and perceived gains are neglected.

These limitations are discussed in turn below.

*Narrow stakeholder identification*    The compromise approach often defines stakeholders in relation to project benefits rather than in terms of preventing or resolving conflicts. For example, the two most common parameters used in stakeholder analysis to grade different groups are:

o   **Importance**: how far is a stakeholder group likely to benefit from the project?
o   **Influence**: how much power and resources does the group have to support or undermine the project's objectives?

These two parameters are useful in determining the 'best-fit' solution to conflict prevention or resolution within the confines of the existing project design. But considering only them may limit the possibility for a more consensual outcome. Other parameters for identifying and grading stakeholders include:

o   **Unintended third parties**: those uninfluential stakeholders who might be inadvertently affected by the project, either positively or negatively.
o   **Assistance**: those organizations (public or private) that might be able to provide compensation or contribute new, creative solutions.

The compromise approach is limited because it is governed by the objective of maximizing project benefits. If this is replaced by the overarching objective of managing conflict, then a far broader range of stakeholder parameters comes into play. Some of these parameters will indeed be about maximizing benefits. But others will be about preventing future conflicts and protecting project benefits in the long term.

*Fixed objectives*   If the various stakeholders' initial objectives are seen as immovable, it is difficult to find win–win outcomes to a conflict. A compromise approach tends to define the stakeholders' initial objectives and then work within these to find the best-fit solution.

In contrast, a consensus approach investigates at a deeper level: the underlying social and economic needs that generate the stakeholders' initial objectives. The approach tries to redefine any conflicting objectives in terms of these underlying needs. It is open to the possibility that some of the stakeholders' underlying needs are the same – and for those needs that do conflict, it assumes that solutions can be found that do not impinge on the exclusive underlying needs of others. This widening of such 'common ground' provides greater scope for win–win solutions.

Box 2.3 gives an example of the importance of exploring underlying needs rather than initial objectives.

*Defining resource use*   A consensus approach to conflict management tries to avoid broad generalizations in the parties' descriptions of the conflict and its prevention or resolution. Because resource conflicts often involve the same general area of land, or the same types of animals or plants, it is not uncommon for the issues to be exaggerated. It is sometimes assumed, for example, that if two different parties use the same resource in the same

---

## Box 2.3.  Example of exploring underlying needs

Two community groups are involved in a land-ownership dispute. For each group, the initial objective is to be declared the sole owner of the disputed area.

A compromise approach to resolving this dispute would assume that these initial objectives are fixed. A solution would be sought that allowed each party to meet some of its expectations. For example, a compromise might involve a trade-off over the area of land to which each group lays claim. A map might be drawn up, with each party achieving part of its objectives.

A consensus approach would be different. It would explore whether the demand for sole land ownership is underpinned by some deeper-seated need that might enable negotiations to move away from the immediate conflict and on to common ground. For example, the investigation might find that both parties wanted to be eligible for revenues when the land was converted to plantation agriculture. If this is known, the negotiations could centre not on land ownership but on the common desire for future revenues. The solution might be to postpone the land ownership issue indefinitely, and agree to divide the revenue between the two groups.

---

area, then this is an unsustainable situation involving incompatible wants or needs. But the details are lacking: where and when the resource is needed, how much is required, how it will be processed. Being specific about these factors often reveals ways the resource can be shared in some mutually compatible way.

*Strategic constraints*   Compromise approaches operate principally within the confines of the strategic elements of a project. These include the location, type, scale and rate of project implementation. Thus many of the parameters of the analysis are already set. There is little flexibility to look outside these strategic components.

*Analysis versus negotiation*   A key difference between a compromise and a consensus approach lies in the degree of negotiation that takes place. Stakeholder analysis, for example, is often a compromise approach based on the gathering of information and the 'engineering' of solutions, usually by one party.

Consensus approaches are less about analysis and engineered solutions, and more about finding solutions through consultation and negotiation. They rely on the creativity that comes from different stakeholders understanding the others' underlying motivations and, on this basis, entering into joint problem solving. The stakeholders, not the analyst, define how the information will be used, and how different groups will be affected by the solutions.

*Perceived mutual gains*   Following on from the above, compromise approaches often fail to explore fully the intangible benefits and losses that different stakeholders perceive will accrue to them from a particular solution. Conventional cost/benefit analysis is one example. This approach assigns monetary values to the different impacts of a solution, so identifying overall winners and losers. Changes are then recommended to minimize the losses or enhance the benefits.

However, cost/benefit analysis can be used more creatively. Community participatory techniques can help to identify the widest possible range of tangible and intangible impacts (i.e. the positive and negative effects on social and environmental capital). Environmental valuation techniques can then be used to attach monetary values to the intangible items. Adding the tangible and intangible costs, and incorporating weightings to address inequity, can minimize overall losses. The aim is to reduce the losses of individual stakeholder groups to the point where all feel they have gained without having to compromise. In the conventional approach, monetary values are not assigned to intangible impacts, so the range of solutions is severely restricted, often precluding a win–win outcome.

29

## Choosing the most practicable strategy

Although consensual negotiations often lead to mutually acceptable and therefore more sustainable outcomes, such an approach may not always be possible (Chupp, 1991). Even where it is possible, it may not be effective on its own; it may require support from other types of conflict management, either at the same time, or beforehand or afterwards. The process of determining the most practicable strategy to adopt will need to take account of a range of factors. Some of these are given in Box 2.4. Figure 2.6 is designed to assist in constructing this strategy.

Where time and resources are limited, and the contributing structural conflicts (land ownership, ethnic disputes, etc.) are insurmountable, the most practicable strategy may be merely to prevent the dispute from escalating or from harming the project.

---

**Box 2.4. Factors in choosing the most practicable strategy**

o The time and resources available for co-ordinating the conflict-management process.

o The likelihood of structural conflicts magnifying the immediate dispute, and the possibility that they can be resolved or managed.

o The power of the different parties to force through their agenda.

o The strength of feeling the conflicting parties have towards each other, and towards achieving their own goals.

o The importance of building or maintaining good relationships between the parties.

o The consequences if the conflict continues, such as escalation towards violence.

o The urgency to manage or resolve the conflict.

o The effectiveness of existing customary, institutional and legal conflict-management mechanisms.

o Those components within the existing customary, institutional or legal mechanisms that could be readily strengthened using conventional methods (force, withdrawal, compromise, accommodation).

o Those components within existing mechanisms that could best be strengthened through consensus building.

o If consensus building is to be used, the principal 'best alternative to a negotiated agreement', i.e. the fallback position if consensual negotiation fails.

---

| Specific strategies | Strategic options |
|---|---|

Force

————————————▶
- ○ Adversarial 'uncompromising' negotiation
- ○ Legal channels
- ○ Electoral system
- ○ Use of mass media to rally support
- ○ Public protest
- ○ Threat of withdrawal
- ○ Lobbying

Withdrawal

————————▶ ◀ · · · · · ·
- ○ Avoidance
- ○ Opting out
- ○ Delaying tactics
- ○ Postponement of decision
- ○ Temporary boycott
- ○ Strikes

Accommodation

————————▶ ◀———
- ○ Relationship dominates
- ○ Goodwill nurtured

Compromise 妥协

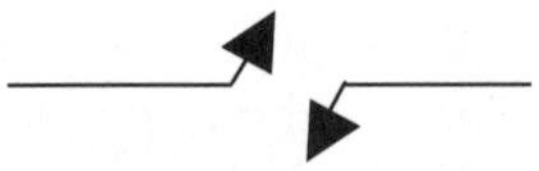

——————▲ ▼———
- ○ Trade-off
- ○ Arbitration

Consensus

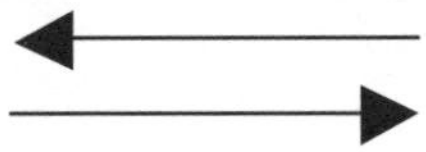

◀—————————
—————————▶
- ○ Direct consensual negotiation (no facilitator)
- ○ Third-party facilitated negotiation

**Figure 2.6** Options for a most practicable strategy for managing conflict

31

# Chapter 3

# What is consensus building?

Consensus building is about facilitating individuals, groups and organizations to adapt to a changing world. The process is a response to the inequalities of confrontational forms of negotiation. It seeks to build the capacity of people to talk with each other, either directly or indirectly, to find a way forward that is based on consensus and that generates mutual gains for all parties with the minimum of compromise and trade-off. Processes of negotiation based on the same principles of mutual gain include alternative conflict management, alternative dispute resolution, conflict resolution and conflict transformation.

## Relevance to livelihood projects

Conflicts between stakeholder groups involved in livelihood projects can be a barrier to project equity, efficiency and sustainability. Poorly designed interventions or community-initiated projects can introduce new conflicts or exacerbate dormant ones. Conversely, projects and interventions that proactively consider the risks posed by conflict can help to reduce existing disputes, prevent new ones arising and provide mechanisms for managing crises that occur during implementation.

Multiple stakeholders and complex issues have meant failure for conventional, adversarial forms of conflict management in development projects. This has generated interest in consensus building. For livelihood projects, consensus building aims to reach agreement between all stakeholder groups. These may include community groups (individuals, informal groups, formal committees, landowners, common resource users, etc.), NGOs, private companies (product and service providers), trade unions, political parties, and local and central government agencies.

## Relevance to peace building

Consensus-building techniques have developed over the past decade as a means to address violent and non-violent conflicts alike. This has created some confusion. For example, in a livelihoods context the word 'conflict' may refer to a dispute over land rights between a lessee and landowner. In a peace-building context, it refers to war, overt violence and large-scale political instability. This book applies consensus building to managing nonviolent disputes, especially those encountered during community-based natural resources and other livelihood projects. The ideas and examples presented here do play a role in peace building, but this is limited to preventing latent conflicts from emerging, or to rehabilitation and reconciliation after violence has subsided. The shaded areas in Figure 3.1 show some of the roles of consensus building in the management of violent conflict.

## Goal of consensus building

The goal of consensus building is to generate agreements and outcomes that are acceptable to all conflicting parties with a minimum of compromise. It aims to achieve a win–win solution, so that each participant is able to describe the outcome as one in which 'I am happy and you are happy'. This contrasts with adversarial approaches to conflict management, such as those common in judicial systems (where one party tends to win and the other lose), or negotiations involving compromise or trade-offs, where all sides try to minimize their losses.

**Figure 3.1.** Role of consensus building in managing violent conflict

At first sight, the likelihood of achieving a win–win outcome from a conflict situation can seem wholly improbable. The conflicting parties often have entrenched positions, are hostile towards one another, and view the other party's demands as totally unacceptable and diametrically opposed to their own. However, human nature is such that these conflict situations carry with them a high degree of perception rather than fact. Consensus building seeks to transform these perceptions by steering the conflicting parties:

○ away from negotiating over their immediate demands, towards addressing the underlying needs that are the true motivating factors behind people's decisions;

○ away from thinking about only one solution, towards considering the widest possible and most creative range of options for meeting the underlying needs; and

○ away from personalized and often exaggerated demands, towards clarity and precision in describing both the underlying needs and the range of proposed options.

## Effectiveness of consensus building

Consensus building is more effective in addressing some types of conflicts than others. For example, it is less useful in resolving underlying structural and identity conflicts than in disputes over declining availability of natural resources. This is shown in broad terms in Figure 3.2. How the process of consensus building might be adapted to address each type of conflict is described in Table 3.1.

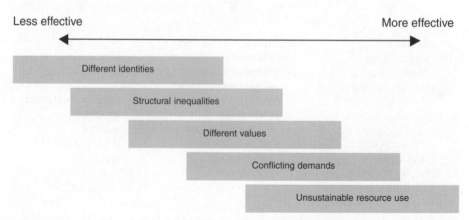

**Figure 3.2.** Effectiveness of consensus-building approaches for different types of conflict

34

Table 3.1. Adaptation of consensus building to different underlying causes of conflict

| Underlying cause of conflict | Adaptations to consensus building to promote effectiveness |
|---|---|
| Unsustainable resource use | ○ Encourage conflicting parties to explore new, more sustainable technological options, including training, new skills and appropriate technologies to raise productivity<br>○ Seek solutions by citing the common need to sustain and improve the resource base |
| Conflicting demands | Most demands are negotiable: the underlying need driving the demand can be satisfied in more ways than are at first obvious:<br>○ Identify a wide range of options for meeting the parties' underlying needs<br>○ Use objective criteria to evaluate the merits of different options<br>○ Formulate integrative solutions |
| Conflicting values | ○ Differing human values may be non-negotiable. However, it may be possible to find common underlying needs or an overriding mutual goal that steers discussion away from the need to resolve different values |
| Structural inequalities | ○ Help disenfranchised groups to understand their own and other parties' perceptions of the conflict<br>○ Aim to transform conflict into a mutual force for social change, so that resolutions are sustainable in the long run<br>○ Use public pressure and involve women to keep the parties at the negotiating table. This approach is best used in conjunction with national-level projects and events |
| Different identities | ○ Emphasize procedural ground rules during negotiations<br>○ Encourage conflicting parties to be specific in their negative perceptions of each other (i.e. not to make generalizations)<br>○ Encourage parties to recall times when they lived without conflict<br>○ Aim to build positive perceptions and solutions |

Adapted from McDonald (1994), Scott et al. (1998), and Moore (1996)

# Best alternative to a negotiated agreement

If the chosen 'most practicable strategy' for conflict management contains some aspect of consensual negotiation, each party must understand its 'best alternative to a negotiated agreement' before entering the process. In other words, what will each party do if the attempt at consensus breaks down? For example, could the party turn to the legal system, use economic or political force, withdraw from the project altogether or concede some of their goals by compromising? Will each party decide to accommodate the others' goals because of some deeper desire to maintain good relations? In short, no party should enter into consensus building without having weighed up the consequences if the process fails to reach agreement.

## Consensus building back in context

Consensus building is not a panacea. It should be used only if it forms part of the most practicable overall strategy. Box 2.4 and Figure 2.6 outlined the range of factors and options that should be considered in constructing this overall strategy.

The next chapter sets out the core principles of consensus building, and the detailed process is described in the chapters that follow.

# Chapter 4

# Principles of consensus building

Consensus building is a process. It may be fairly rapid, for example when used to manage a minor dispute, or it may span many months, even years, involving the building of rapport, consultations at both government and community levels, various types of community participatory analysis, the strengthening of customary conflict-management mechanisms, and the training of community leaders in modern facilitation and negotiation skills. Various stages in the process of consensus building are discussed in Chapters 5 to 11.

This chapter discusses ten principles that underpin the process of consensus building (Figure 4.1). In practice, these principles may overlap, and different principles should be emphasized at different stage in the process. How this works will depend on the type of conflict, the type of consensual negotiations that take place, and the participants' and facilitators' skills and experience.

## Accommodate cultural differences

Understanding the cultural differences between conflicting parties is a prime factor in working out how best to manage a conflict. The parties may have different expectations and attitudes, both towards the conflict itself and how it should be handled. These differences may not only hinder the consensual negotiations, they may also lead to profound misunderstanding and escalation.

In the highlands of Papua New Guinea, for example, some people see violence not as a problem but as a means of resolving conflicts. In other places, some place great importance on verbal agreements, while others, for example private firms, respect only legally binding documents. In the Fiji Islands, for example, some logging companies have reached what indi-genous Fijian groups thought were satisfactory verbal agreements over the distribution of profits, only to find that the companies did not see this as a culturally acceptable way of doing business.

Cultural differences are especially important where conventional ways of managing a conflict have broken down. Examples are where village youths

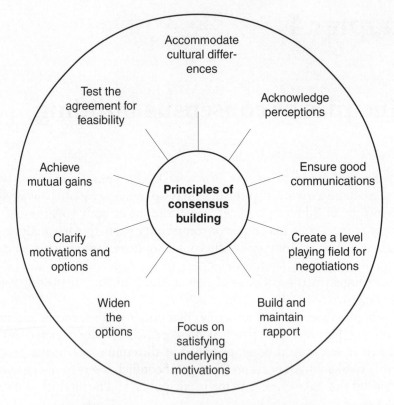

**Figure 4.1.** Principles of consensus building

## TRAINING EXERCISE 4.1.  CULTURAL DIFFERENCES

### Objective
To understand how cultural differences between the key stakeholder groups can affect consensual negotiations.

### Tasks
1.  For a conflict they are all familiar with, ask the participants individually to identify two or three of the key stakeholder groups.
2.  Map the cultural differences of each stakeholder group against the criteria in Box 4.1.
3.  In plenary, discuss whether these differences might obstruct negotiations. If so, how might they be accommodated?

## Box 4.1.   Common conflict-related cultural differences

○ **Attitude to conflict**   What each party feels towards conflict (dispute or violence) in general: positive, to be avoided, etc.

○ **Communication style**   How each party communicates information and ideas, and the potential this holds for misunderstandings.

○ **Willingness to disclose**   How comfortable each party is in stating objectives, discussing emotions, acknowledging fears, needing to save face, etc.

○ **Method of reasoning**   How each party solves problems: quantitative information, qualitative information, personal experience, examples, case studies, theories, proven principles, reciprocity, payback, leaders' opinions.

○ **Decision making**   How each party reaches a collective decision: voting, consensus, autocracy, etc.

○ **Acceptable outcomes**   What form an agreement has to take for it to be acceptable to each party: legal judgement, verbal agreement, written contract, approval of a particular individual or institution, etc.

no longer respect traditional mechanisms, one party cannot access the legal system or arbitration is politically manipulated. In such cases, systematic consensus building may be justified.

In introducing the consensus-building approach, a key decision is whether to build on existing mechanisms or to establish new, independent ones. A factor in this decision is the cultural diversity of the stakeholder groups – their different views of conflict and how to manage it.

Box 4.1 lists some of the cultural characteristics that may differ between indigenous groups, settlers, government agencies, firms, donors and other parties. Using these criteria to appraise the main stakeholder groups will give an idea of their cultural diversity.

High levels of cultural diversity can derive from many sources: diverse ethnic cultures (as in the highlands of Papua New Guinea), diverse social status (as in mixed-caste communities in southern India) and diverse livelihood strategies (e.g. the gift economies of the rural poor and the market orientation of the wealthier poor and of private firms).

Following this analysis, two general rules can be applied for managing conflicts:

○ Where cultural diversity is low, try first to strengthen conventional mechanisms of managing the conflict, be they customary, institutional or legal.

○ Where cultural diversity is high, consider developing independent mechanisms. As far as practicable, these mechanisms should contain elements familiar to all parties, such as a third-party impartial facilitator, or agreements based on consensus.

## Acknowledge perceptions

Whether one is a mediator or one of the disputing parties, it is important to acknowledge and understand the perceptions of the different stakeholder groups. Perceptions rather than facts often drive people's decisions. In a conflict, it is important not to begin by challenging a party's perceptions, but to appreciate that these perceptions are very real – in that they have real effects. Conflicts tend to carry strong emotions, so arguments are unlikely to change initial perceptions, especially if they are strengthened and validated by a wider group.

A principle of consensus building is to understand and acknowledge, without prejudice, how each stakeholder perceives the causes and significance of the conflict.

The word 'understand' here means 'comprehend', not 'agree with'. Knowledge is power: a party's power depends on its ability to put itself in another party's shoes (Fisher et al., 1994).

A word of warning: it is tempting for a facilitator to learn about people's perceptions by asking them to tell stories about the conflict, its causes and the feelings it generates. Some conflict-management practitioners see storytelling as vital. But it is no panacea. Sometimes storytelling is necessary, as in some forms of post-conflict reconciliation (South Africa's Truth and Reconciliation Commission is an example). However, storytelling may just reinforce adversarial positions. As Fisher et al. (1994, p. 35) argue, 'the more a position is worked out in detail and the more often it is repeated, the more committed to it a party becomes. Focusing on the other side's position is likely to structure a situation as a contest of will in which an objective becomes not to budge.'

Avoid the arrogance of saying, 'if they knew what we know, then they would not be demanding these things'. NGOs, private firms, government agencies and other outsiders often have such attitudes, based on what they see as their superior technology and knowledge. But such perceptions can blind the outsiders to what may be very valid reasons for community groups behaving the way they do. The extensive literature on community participation covers techniques for analysing and working with indigenous technical knowledge and community perspectives (Chambers, 1997).

## Ensure good communications

In consensual negotiations, co-ordinators, facilitator and participants must develop and maintain good communications with all those involved. Part of this communication will be to convey one party's perceptions to the others, in a way that is faithful to that party.

**TRAINING EXERCISE 4.2.   LISTENING SKILLS**

**Objective**

To develop better listening skills.

**Tasks**

1.  Divide the participants into pairs.
2.  Ask one person in each pair to speak to the other on an issue he or she is passionate about.
3.  Instruct the listener to sit opposite the speaker but to act uninterested and to refrain from making any comment.
4.  The speaker is allowed to talk for one minute – no more. (Keep this information secret from the participants.)
5.  Once the minute is up, ask the speaker to repeat the same speech, but this time the listener must use all his or her communication skills: eye contact, body language, nodding in agreement, asking questions, seeking clarifications, etc.
6.  The speaker and listener swap roles and repeat the exercise using a different topic.

Source: S. Jones, University of Wolverhampton

Good communication is also about having good personal skills. Minor personal skills include the ability to listen (see Training Exercise 4.2), positive body language, punctuality and honesty.

More practised skills include recognizing different patterns of behaviour in oneself and in others (see Training Exercise 4.3) and employing appropriate assertiveness.

# Create a level playing field

One of the factors in genuine collaborative negotiations is that all parties enter the process on a level playing field. Each party should have an equal capacity to understand the dynamics of the conflict, explain its perceptions, understand the other parties' perceptions and to take part constructively in consensual negotiations.

Facilitators may need to allocate time and resources to raising the most disenfranchised parties' capacity to negotiate. Participatory rural appraisal (PRA) is one way of doing this at the community level. Other techniques include training community representatives in negotiation skills, and raising the awareness of government agencies and firms about the value of consensus to improve a project's long-term sustainability.

# TRAINING EXERCISE 4.3.   BUILDING TRUST

## Objective
To learn about developing trust so that stakeholder groups can exchange and share their ideas.

## Tasks
1. Explain the diagram below to the participants (diagram adapted from the 'Johari window').

| | |
|---|---|
| **1   Common knowledge**<br>Things we know about ourselves that the other stakeholders also know about us | **2   Blind knowledge**<br>Things we do not know about ourselves that other stakeholders do know |
| **3   Secret knowledge**<br>Things we know about ourselves but would not like other stakeholders to know | **4   Missing knowledge**<br>Things we do not know about ourselves and other stakeholders do not know either |

2. Divide participants into small groups.
3. One member of the group describes to the others a past conflict situation with which he/she is familiar (this could be a domestic disagreement, work-related dispute, conflict within a development project, etc.).
4. The group assumes the role of one of the stakeholders in the conflict.
5. Assuming that the conflict has just come to light, the group writes down three items for each of the four windows in the diagram.
6. The group identifies ways that items in windows 2, 3 and 4 could be shifted to window 1.
7. In plenary session, the groups present their findings and the lessons learned.

Source: Adapted from PEACE Foundation Melanesia (1998)

# Build and maintain rapport

Good relations with the different stakeholders are essential both for both the facilitator and the negotiating parties themselves. It is not by mere coincidence that firms hire pleasant, approachable staff to manage their public relations activities. But approachability is just one ingredient of building good rapport. Other ingredients include:

o   listening;
o   finding common points of interest;
o   developing trust;
o   using the local (or another appropriate) language;
o   sharing experiences;
o   acknowledging different values; and
o   treating others with respect.

Good rapport can quickly turn into friendship and from there into favouritism – either apparent or real. Perceived favouritism can generate jealousy and mistrust, and can undermine consensual negotiation. For this reason, all parties should keep relations professional and non-personal. This applies especially to facilitators and mediators who wish to remain impartial.


# Focus on satisfying underlying motivations

Probably the most fundamental principle of consensual negotiation is to investigate the parties' underlying motivations – their deeper interests, social and cultural values, ethnic identify, basic welfare and livelihood needs, their desire for face-saving, social inclusion and moral justice, their access to income, loss of power, etc. These interests lie beneath an individual's or party's more immediate positions and demands. If they are understood, perhaps creative ways can be found to satisfy them and so reduce the conflict. For every underlying motivation there usually exists a range of options that might satisfy it –not just the first one expressed and argued for. The problem is that these first articulations usually define the first stage of a conflict. Consensual negotiations should therefore draw the conflicting parties away from their immediate demands towards a broader discussion about how to satisfy their underlying motivations.

Two types of underlying motivations are usually present in a conflict:
o   **Common underlying motivations**   This is where two or more of the conflicting parties share the same motivation. For example, a dispute between different community groups over the use of communal forest resources might be underlain by the common need to sustain the forest into the future, increase social status or generate income.

43

o **Individual underlying motivations**   Stakeholder groups may have very specific – and very different – underlying motivations. Sometimes these will be incompatible with those of others. However, it may be possible to find solutions to these needs that do not impinge on the underlying motivations of others. Rather than one party's individual underlying motivations being sidelined, it is better to try to find creative solutions to satisfy them.

In general, it is easier to search for solutions by starting with common underlying motivations. This helps maintain momentum towards consensus. It may also coincidentally address some of the parties' individual underlying needs, thus avoiding the need to confront them directly. Once some common ground has been found, work can begin on the search for solutions to individual needs. Figure 4.2 illustrates the value of concentrating on underlying motivations rather than immediate demands.

## Widen the options

Widening the options through joint problem solving is the second fundamental principle of consensus building (identifying underlying motivations being the first).

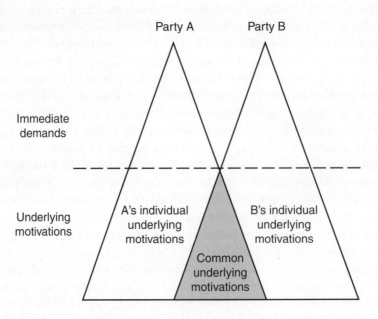

**Figure 4.2.**   Satisfying underlying motivations

Too many people enter negotiations with only one demand or solution in mind. They have identified the position they wish to take, rather than the underlying motivations they want to satisfy. This can quickly lead to an impasse. As Fisher et al. (1994, p. 5) argue, consensus building:

> '...is a paradigm shift away from a conception of conflict and negotiation that stresses static substantive solutions and towards an approach that stresses the power of process. Rarely is a conflict intractable simply because no one has a good idea of how things ought to be... In most cases the difficulty lies not in a lack of potential substantive options but in a failure to design, negotiate and pursue a process that moves us forward from where we are now to where we would like to be.'

Consensual negotiation involves pursuing mutually acceptable win–win outcomes by encouraging the conflicting parties to analyse their underlying motivations and widen the range of options for satisfying them. Widening the options can begin with brainstorming with individual parties and develop further by drawing on the collective creativity of all the parties through joint problem solving.

This involves skills usually absent from adversarial approaches to conflict management: creativity, brainstorming and lateral thinking.


## Creativity

Different stakeholders are often unable to move forward: they get stuck. Creative thinking helps get things moving again. The problems arise because:

o   The parties do not know what they want.
o   They believe that the only solutions are those currently in front of them.
o   They do not realize the possible long-term negative consequences of achieving their demands.

People may get stuck because they think in patterns that limit the actions that can be taken (see Training Exercise 4.4). Conventional benefit/cost analysis is an example of this. Creative thinking moves outside these restrictive patterns.


## Brainstorming

The word 'brainstorming' covers a range of methods designed to stimulate creativity and generate a wide range of options. Participants begin by brainstorming individually, for example by writing down a list of ideas. They then move to working in small groups. Finally the ideas are amalgamated in plenary and a discussion is held to try to be even more creative and widen the options still further.

One benefit of brainstorming is that when the parties all perceive that every possible option has been identified, they will become more realistic about what can be achieved: there is nowhere else to turn but the options before them.

See Chapter 15 for how to manage a brainstorming session.

## TRAINING EXERCISE 4.4.   CONVENTIONAL PATTERNS

### Objective
To demonstrate the importance of thinking outside of conventional patterns.

### Tasks
1.  Draw a 3 × 3 matrix of nine dots, like this:

2.  Tell the participants to join all the dots with no more than four straight lines, but without taking their pens off the page.
3.  Compare the answers to the solution below:

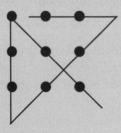

4.  Discuss with participants whether there is a way to join all the dots with a single straight line. (Answer: Fold the paper until all dots are positioned one above each other, then push a pen through the dots and paper.)

## Lateral thinking

Edward De Bono (1999) has put forward a number of techniques to help people structure their thinking processes. He calls this 'lateral thinking'. His 'six thinking hats' is one example. Each hat represents a different way to think about a subject.

o   **White hat**   White suggests paper. The white hat concerns information. When we consciously put on the white hat, we ask ourselves questions such as: 'What information do we have?', 'What information do we need?', 'What questions should we be asking?' The white hat draws our attention to what we know and what we do not know.

o   **Green hat**   Green suggests energy and life. The green hat is for creativity and new ideas. When we wear our green hat, we try to be as creative as we can.

o   **Black hat**   Black suggests authority and judgement. The black hat is for caution. When we put on the black hat, we evaluate ideas to look for the weaknesses, limitations and dangers.

o   **Yellow hat**   Yellow suggests sunshine and optimism. The yellow hat stimulates us to look for the positive aspects of the matter in hand. When we are wearing the yellow hat, we explore the benefits and advantages of an idea.

o   **Red hat**   Red suggests fire and warmth. The red hat is to do with feelings, intuition and emotions. When we put on the red hat, we explore our feelings about the matter.

o   **Blue hat**   Blue suggests water and reflection. The blue hat is for managing the whole thinking process by reflecting on where we are, where we want to be and what we need to do next. When we choose the blue hat, we are signalling a period of review and summary.

Of course, it is not necessary to have to wear (or talk about) coloured hats to think in a particular way. The hats need only suggest a particular way to approach a negotiation and formulate questions (see Training Exercise 4.5).

## Clarify underlying motivations and options

In Chapter 2, we identified the importance of transforming conflicts from matters of perception and exaggeration into matters of fact. This is part of the overall idea of 'reframing'. (Another key aspect of reframing is the transformation of negative perceptions into the search for solutions. For example: *Participant* – 'All this talk is getting us nowhere.' *Facilitator* – 'It sounds as though rapid progress is important to you. What would signify to you that we were really making progress?')

47

## TRAINING EXERCISE 4.5.   LATERAL THINKING

### Objective
To learn how to structure questions to assist lateral thinking.

### Tasks
1.  Divide participants into pairs.
2.  Ask one of the pair to select a conflict situation he or she is familiar with.
3.  The other person selects a 'hat' (other than blue), and within that mode puts questions to his or her partner. The questions should explore the underlying motivations driving one of the stakeholders in the conflict.
4.  After ten minutes, the questioner chooses a different hat and carries on questioning. If time allows, the questioner continues working through the different hats.
5.  End the exercise with the blue hat, which is about reflection and planning a way forward.
6.  In plenary, discuss the results and the relative utility of the different hats. Which mode worked best, and why?

Encouraging the different parties to be specific about their views of a conflict helps consensual negotiations since it often opens the way to a wider range of solutions. In particular, disputing parties should be encouraged to be clear and precise about their underlying motivations and possible ways to manage the conflict. Such precision will be possible only if sufficient rapport has been built up, and if the parties' perceptions have first been acknowledged without prejudice.

## Clarifying underlying motivations

It may be safer first to consult with each stakeholder group independently, rather than in a workshop or plenary meeting. The facilitator can then ask for permission to explain these motivations to the other parties. If time is short, and if mutual rapport is particularly good, it may be possible to conduct these sessions with all participants together.

Some common clarification questions are:
o   'Very briefly, what is the problem here?' Ask the participants to be brief, preventing them from focusing on negative aspects and inflaming others.
o   Digging a little deeper: 'Why is it a problem?'

## TRAINING EXERCISE 4.6.    CLARIFICATION I
## (ORANGE NEGOTIATIONS)

### Objective

To learn some of the clarification skills used in consensual negotiation.

### Tasks

1.   Divide the participants into pairs.
2.   Allocate one person in each pair to each of the characters in the briefing notes in Appendix 1.
3.   Instruct the participants to role-play the negotiation process outlined in the briefing notes. Do not allow the participants to see each other's notes. The objective is to arrive at a consensus, i.e. a win–win outcome. Ask each pair to record the outcome.
4.   In plenary, the participants report the outcomes of their negotiations.
5.   Discuss the different types of outcomes, for example: those that focused on the number of oranges or the price to be paid versus those that realized that one party wanted to use the juice, while the other needed only the skin.
6.   Discuss the relevance of how questions were asked during the negotiations and the importance of clarifying the other side's underlying motivations in detail.

## TRAINING EXERCISE 4.7.    CLARIFICATION II
## (MINING AND WILDLIFE RESERVE)

### Objective

To strengthen clarification skills used in consensual negotiation.

### Tasks

1.   Run through steps 1 to 5 in Training Exercise 4.6 again, this time using the briefing notes in Appendix 2.
2.   Emphasize to the participants the importance of: (a) exploring each others' underlying motivations; (b) identifying both the common and individual needs (see Figure 4.2); and (c) using clarification questions to create room for finding a win–win solution. After the negotiations, explain that one party wanted only to explore the lower reaches of the reserve while the other wanted to protect the upper reaches.

o   If the underlying motivations are still elusive, try 'Why is this a prob-
    lem?' (again), or 'What exactly is behind this concern?'
o   Then: 'Do you think this fundamental problem is shared by any of the
    other stakeholder groups?'

Now try to clarify the detail. For example, ask:
o   Where exactly (in terms of geography) does this motivation apply?
o   Who is involved? How many people are involved?
o   What is the timing? (urgent, within six months, before a critical date,
    etc.)
o   What principles are involved in meeting the motivation?
o   Are there any inherent assumptions or risks?

### Clarifying options

A similar approach is taken to clarifying promising options. After options have been brainstormed and the most promising ones taken forward, these priorities should be clarified – spatially, temporally and
quantitatively. This gives them credibility and prevents false expectations arising later.

## Achieve mutual gains

The purpose of exploring the stakeholders' underlying motivations and then
widening the options is to enable a consensus where each stakeholder perceives that his or her group has benefited. This outcome of perceived mutual gain is the goal of consensus building. It is what sets consensus building apart from other types of conflict-resolution strategies.

The approach is possible because consensual negotiations explicitly try
to increase the basis upon which decisions can be reached. They try to change
the rules of the game in previously unimagined ways. This may mean discussing new technologies, redefining ways resources are accessed (e.g. by
extending land leases), changing attitudes to others' behaviour and cultures, and enabling people to save face. Above all, solutions are needed
that overtake the immediate concerns, leaving them redundant. When time
for a settlement comes, the pie should be substantially larger than before
(Figure 4.3).

Contradictory as it may seem, it is precisely because the parties are in
conflict that a win–win outcome is possible. The greater the conflict, the
more entrenched are people's positions, so the more scope there is to widen
the basis for agreement. It is by slowly broadening people's understanding
of their own and others' demands, and encouraging them to think outside

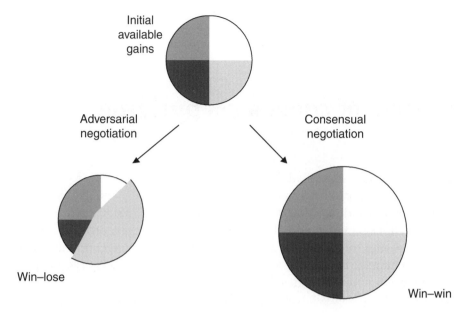

**Figure 4.3.** Concept of achieving mutual gains

their entrenched and emotional positions, that win–win outcomes are entirely plausible.

## Test the agreement for feasibility

Amidst the enthusiasm surrounding the final stages of consensual negotiation, it is easy to forget to test the feasibility of the agreement. Some of the feasibility issues should already have been addressed during clarification activities. But the final agreement must be tested again before it can be accepted.

Here are some questions to consider when testing for feasibility.

o   Does each party have realistic expectations of the agreement?
o   Are the options technically feasible?
o   Is adequate finance available?
o   Is the timetable feasible?
o   Will the agreement result in rapid gains or in milestones that will maintain momentum for longer-term changes?
o   Do the negotiators have the support of the people they represent?
o   Is the agreement politically viable?
o   Is the agreement socially desirable and environmentally sustainable?
o   Are mechanisms in place to ensure that each party maintains its side of the agreement?

# Chapter 5

# Process of consensus building

Once it has been established that the most practicable strategy to manage a conflict will include consensus building (see Chapter 2), the facilitator and parties must decide how to do this. The process will be different in every case. It will also evolve and change over time. However, certain components are part of most consensus-building processes. This is so whether the goal is to manage conflicts that arise within existing projects or to integrate conflict-prevention strategies during project design.

Figure 5.1 shows the key building blocks of consensus building.

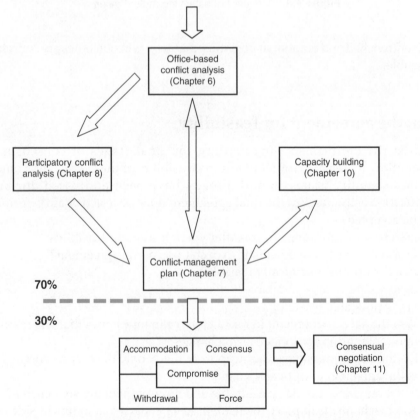

**Figure 5.1.** Building blocks of consensus building

The process does not happen in a strict sequence. For example, it is necessary to identify the different stakeholders' underlying motivations. This can be done at the beginning (as an office-based study), as an early exercise in the consensual negotiation itself, or both. Similarly, capacity building – strengthening the skills of disenfranchised groups – may be integral to participatory analysis, or may be done through a dedicated training programme.

Despite this, a general sequence is recognizable. It is usual, and safest, to analyse a conflict situation before engaging people in consensual negotiations, and before deciding what capacity building may be needed to enable the negotiations to be effective.

It is also common for conflict analysis to be done in two stages. First, the conflict is analysed 'in the office', on the basis of existing or readily accessed information. From this, a provisional conflict-management plan can be made. This outlines the most practicable strategy to adopt, the steps to take next and the capacity-building measures to undertake. Second, the conflict is analysed in participation with the relevant stakeholder groups. This analysis is used to revise the conflict-management plan. The analysis is repeated, if necessary, until the parties are able to agree to the plan. This process will sometimes include some form of capacity building, for example to enable understanding of others' objectives, training in negotiation skills and to raise awareness of the long-term benefits of consensus.

The conflict analysis, conflict-management plan and capacity building explore all possible avenues to maximize the potential for a win–win outcome and minimize the possibility of inadvertently fuelling the conflict. Once these are complete, consensual negotiations can begin.

Figure 5.1 suggests that 70 per cent of the time and effort should go into the first three activities, and 30 per cent for the consensual negotiation phase. These figures are indicative only. It is important not to rush into negotiations without enough preparatory work.

Consensual negotiations can take a number of forms: direct face-to-face discussions between stakeholder groups; facilitation by one of the stakeholder groups; or facilitation by an impartial third party.

The following chapters describe how to undertake these various activities, and offer a variety of tools and techniques for doing so. The tools are divided into those for:

o    office-based conflict analysis (Chapter 6);
o    provisional conflict-management plan (Chapter 7);
o    participatory conflict analysis (Chapters 8 and 9);
o    capacity building (Chapter 10);
o    consensual negotiation (Chapter 11).

Where relevant, exercises have been included in the text, and case studies from Fiji, Bolivia and Papua New Guinea are used as illustrations.

# Chapter 6

# Office-based conflict analysis

Office-based conflict analysis is the research phase of consensus building. It involves mapping the actual or potential conflict (or conflicts) based on information already available or which can be readily gathered. Outputs of this phase include:

o An initial mapping of the conflict: its type, scale and any cause or effect relationships.
o The historical context of the conflict: its past and possible future escalation, its underlying structural causes, the relative contributions of structural causes and development pressures, past efforts at conflict management and why they failed.
o Any current or planned peace-building initiatives that may be relevant.
o For projects currently affected by conflict, the impacts on the project schedule, activities, outputs, assets, staff time, beneficiaries, etc.
o The possible effects of other projects on the goal, purpose and assumptions of this project.
o The geographical distribution of known or possible conflicts.
o The distribution of conflicts over time: seasonal, election-related, etc.
o Prioritization of the conflict in terms of urgency and significance: the need to prevent, manage or resolve it, and the likelihood of it undermining the project's goal.
o For the prioritized conflict(s), the key stakeholder groups and potential representatives of each group.
o An estimate of the initial positions and demands of the different stakeholders, and of their underlying motivating values, interests, needs and concerns.
o An initial identification of how the project might conflict with these positions and underlying motivations.

Based on these characteristics, some possible ways of managing the conflict should be identified:

o Areas of common ground between the stakeholders: e.g. present or past local institutions, common customary mechanisms to managing disputes, common values, underlying motivations, interests, needs or concerns.

o   Cases where the underlying motivations of particular stakeholders might be met without harming the interests of other stakeholders.
o   Cases where certain stakeholders might accept compromise or trade-off.
o   Cases where the project is willing to make concessions in order to maintain good relations.
o   Cases where the project might use force (or threaten to do so).

Some tools for achieving these outputs are described below.

## Initial conflict mapping

A conflict is often more complex than it first seems. It may be related to other disputes, either causing the immediate conflict or caused by it. These disputes may in turn be the result of deeper, structural problems. This complexity needs to be understood. It is possible that the immediate conflict is the only one that needs attention. On the other hand, trying to manage a single dispute may be of little use because it is intertwined with wider problems.

### TRAINING EXERCISE 6.1.   INITIAL CONFLICT MAPPING

**Objective**
To build an understanding of how conflicts interrelate.

**Tasks**
1.   Divide the participants into small groups.
2.   Ask one member of each group to choose a community-based natural resource project where conflict has become an issue. Only one person in the group need know about the project; the others can ask him or her questions about it.
3.   Each group lists the different conflicts going on in this project at a particular time.
4.   The groups identify conflicts that may arise in the future. Examples are those that have emerged from time to time, those known to be dormant, those that are to do with structural inequalities and those that may result from new economic pressures.
5.   The groups draw these conflicts as circles, with the size representing the scale of the conflict. Overlap the circles where the conflicts interrelate. Use dotted circles to denote future conflicts.

Initial conflict mapping uses Venn diagrams, drawn to show how an initial conflict interacts with other disputes (Figure 6.1). The size of the circles represents the relative magnitude of each conflict. The interdependency of the conflicts is represented by the extent to which the circles overlap. Where the conflict is potential rather than actual, this is shown by a dotted line. For projects in their planning phase, the same exercise would distinguish between current conflicts and those that might be stimulated by the project.

In Figure 6.1, the overall perspective taken is that of an NGO involved in the project. The sizes of the circles reflect the degree to which each dispute adversely affects the NGO's project aims.

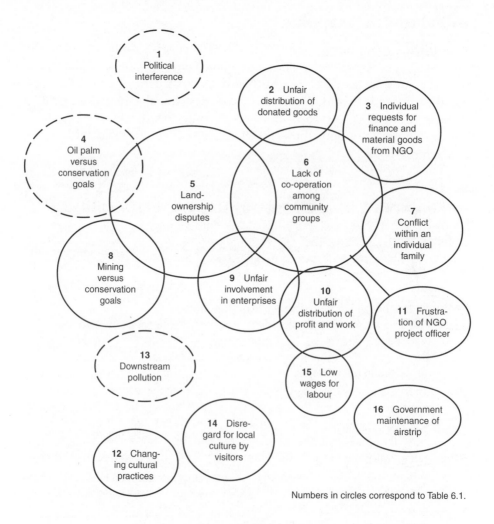

Numbers in circles correspond to Table 6.1.

**Figure 6.1.** Example of initial conflict mapping (integrated conservation and development project, upland Papua New Guinea)

# Spatial conflict mapping

Spatial mapping provides some detail to the initial conflict mapping. It is especially useful in community-based natural resource projects. At this early stage, it is usually enough to draw a sketch map and to mark the areas affected by each conflict. This map will need to be revised through consultation with the affected stakeholders (see Chapter 8).

Figure 6.2 refers to a community-based ecoforestry project in Fiji that involved forest management by land-owning groups using portable sawmills, timber processing and product marketing. In this example, the project was in its late planning stages. The conflicts mapped were those that the sponsoring NGO predicted with the current project design.

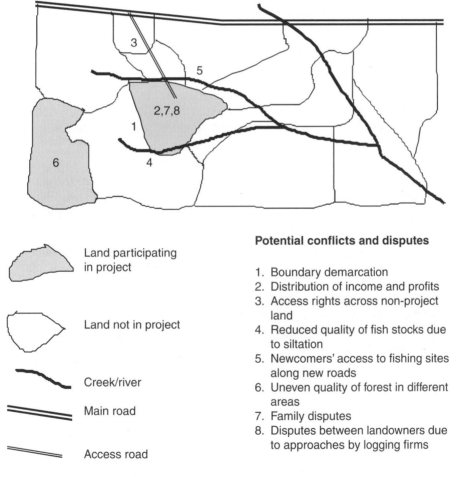

**Potential conflicts and disputes**

Land participating in project

Land not in project

Creek/river

Main road

Access road

1. Boundary demarcation
2. Distribution of income and profits
3. Access rights across non-project land
4. Reduced quality of fish stocks due to siltation
5. Newcomers' access to fishing sites along new roads
6. Uneven quality of forest in different areas
7. Family disputes
8. Disputes between landowners due to approaches by logging firms

**Figure 6.2.** Example of spatial conflict mapping (community ecoforestry project, Fiji Islands)

## Prioritization of conflicts

Whether analysing actual conflicts or predicting future ones, it will be necessary to focus consensus building on those that are most urgent and most significant.

o   **Urgent conflicts** are those that need to be addressed within a certain timeframe. For example, resolving disputes over which community groups should be given technical training may be critical if the donor requires that all training be completed before the grant is released.
o   **Significant conflicts** are those that will significantly threaten the project's success if they are not resolved. For example, a conflict that leads to roadblocks on logging access roads may physically prevent a project's progress. Other conflicts may undermine the project's goals of livelihood sustainability. An example might be where a group of participants decides to sell out and allow unsustainable commercial harvesting.

Many conflicts share some aspects of both urgency and significance. The analysis must identify the urgency and significance of conflicts in relation to each other. It should also reveal whether the conflict is actually benefiting the project or is likely to be resolved by customary conflict-resolution practices, and therefore should be left alone.

Table 6.1 shows the results of a prioritization exercise undertaken for the project in Papua New Guinea (Figure 6.1). The conflicts identified as priorities are shown in **bold**. Note that these are not necessarily the conflicts that show the highest degree of urgency or significance. As with any scoring and ranking exercise, the process of undertaking the exercise is more important than the score or rank itself. A skilled social analyst will stand back from a completed exercise and deliberate on the totality of the experience before gauging the priorities.

**Table 6.1.  Example of a conflict prioritization exercise (integrated conservation and development project, Papua New Guinea)**

| Conflict | | Urgent | Significant |
|---|---|---|---|
| 1 | Political influence: | | |
| | Local level | | * |
| | Provincial level | * | ** |
| | National | * | *** |
| 2 | Unequal distribution of donated goods | *** | * |
| 3 | Individual requests for finance and material goods from NGO | *** | ** |
| **4** | **Oil palm versus conservation goals** | *** | *** |
| 5 | Land ownership disputes: | | |
| | **Research station** | ** | *** |
| | Ecotourism project land | | ** |
| | Tekadu guesthouse | | * |
| 6 | Lack of co-operation between community groups: | | |
| | In community work | *** | *** |
| | **In project-related activities** | *** | ** |
| 7 | Individual family disputes | * | *** |
| 8 | Mining versus conservation goals | * | ** |
| 9 | Unfair involvement in enterprises | ** | *** |
| 10 | Unfair distribution of profit and work: | | |
| | **Kokoro guesthouse** | *** | ** |
| | Ivimka guesthouse | *** | *** |
| | Tekadu guesthouse | * | ** |
| | Okavai guesthouse | | *** |
| | Butterfly farming | | * |
| 11 | Frustration of NGO project officer | | |
| 12 | Changing cultural practices | * | *** |
| 13 | Downstream pollution | * | ** |
| 14 | Disregard for local culture by visitors | | *** |
| 15 | Low wages for labour | *** | ** |
| 16 | Government maintenance of airstrip | *** | * |

Conflicts identified as priorities are shown in **bold**. Numbers correspond to Figure 6.1.

# Stakeholder identification

Effective consensus building depends on engaging all the different stakeholder groups relevant to a conflict or potential conflict. Accurately identifying who these stakeholders are is therefore important. It may not be possible to identify all the relevant groups during the office analysis. Many will not emerge until later, during consultation in the field. However, it is a good idea to start stakeholder identification early, for the following reasons.

*Forward planning*   Plan whom to talk to, and in what order, when the analysis moves from the office to the field. The rationale here is: (a) to avoid inflaming the dispute, for example by ignoring cultural protocol or seeming to favour a particular group; and (b) to optimize subsequent activities within the time and budget available.

*Stakeholder groups and representatives*   Identify obvious groups of stakeholders, and the people who might legitimately represent them.

*Difficult people*   Identify any individuals and groups who are likely to pose particular problems. Think also of how they might be brought into the consensual negotiation. See Chapter 14 for how to deal with such people.

*Positive influence*   Build a picture of any individuals and organizations that are not directly involved in the conflict but that might be able to help manage or resolve it.

*Negative influence*   Likewise, identify those individuals and organizations that are not directly involved, but have the power and influence to undermine an agreement by the main conflicting parties.

   The stakeholder identification should begin with the highest-priority conflict(s). Brainstorming (see Chapter 15) can be used to identify each of the following stakeholder categories:

o   Groups **causing** the conflict (i.e. that are being blamed for the problem).
o   Groups **affected by** the conflict. These may or may not be the same as above. They may be directly or indirectly affected, either positively or negatively.
o   Groups that can help **manage or resolve** the conflict (e.g. by contributing new ideas or financial assistance).
o   Groups that might (for reasons of jealousy, economics, status, political economy, etc.) try to **undermine** the process of conflict management.

## TRAINING EXERCISE 6.3. PRIORITIZING CONFLICTS

### Objective
To prioritize conflicts in order to develop a plan for consensual negotiation.

### Tasks
1. Divide the participants into the same groups as used for Training Exercises 6.1 and 6.2.
2. Ask them to clarify within their groups what is meant by 'urgent' and 'significant' conflicts.
3. For the same project as in Training Exercise 6.1, the participants should develop a matrix similar to the example in Table 6.1. (For projects in their planning phases, most conflicts will require only analysis of 'significance').
4. Once the matrix is complete, instruct the participants to take a short break, then return to agree the priority areas for consensual negotiation.
5. The participants present and justify their priority areas in plenary.

Figure 6.3 provides a form for compiling the results of this exercise. Figure 6.4 shows an example from an agroforestry project in Bolivia, which shows the relationships between the various stakeholders.

Sometimes, a single person or family has to be considered as a stakeholder group in their own right. However, it will usually be possible to find groupings of like-minded people. When sufficient rapport has been built, these may well accept a single representative to speak for them.

Be careful not to confuse these individual stakeholders with 'difficult' people. Individual stakeholders have a unique and legitimate stake in a conflict. Difficult people are those who share the same demands as other

| Causing/blamed for conflict | | Affected by conflict | | May help manage/ resolve conflict | | May undermine conflict management | |
|---|---|---|---|---|---|---|---|
| Stake-holder group | Repre-sentative | Stake-holder group | Repre-sentative | Stake-holder group | Repre-sentative | Stake-holder group | Repre-sentative |
| | | | | | | | |

**Figure 6.3.** Form for compiling the results of stakeholder identification

61

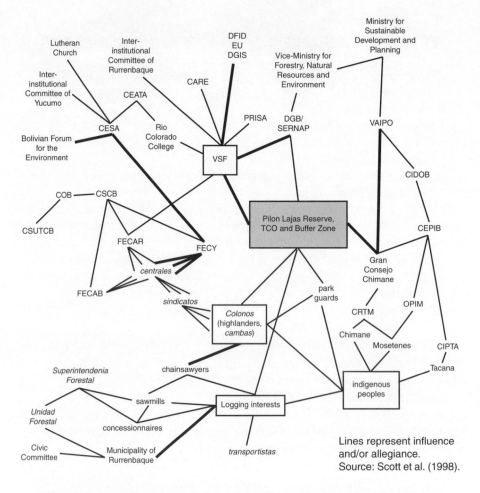

**Figure 6.4.** Mapping of stakeholders (Pilon Lajas agroforestry project, Bolivia)

stakeholders, but who have the personality or power to have a voice of their own. The task will be to find a way to bring them under the same grouping as others with a similar stake (see Chapter 14).

## Underlying motivations

Once the stakeholders relevant to a conflict have been identified, it is necessary to understand them. Numerous issues relating to each stakeholder might be studied: importance, power and influence, objectives, motivations, underlying needs and fears, goals, trade-offs, distributional impacts, equity, political feasibility, compensation, mitigation, etc. Depending on the type of conflict, all or some of these issues may be relevant.

# TRAINING EXERCISE 6.4.
# STAKEHOLDER IDENTIFICATION

## Objective
To identify the stakeholder groups relevant to consensual negotiation.

## Tasks
1. Divide the participants into small groups.
2. One member of the group selects a project that has actual or potential conflicts. This can be the same project as in Training Exercise 6.3.
3. The group selects one urgent or significant conflict relevant to the project. Only one person in the group need know about the conflict; the others can ask questions about it.
4. The participants brainstorm the different stakeholders relevant to the conflict, using the form in Figure 6.3. Ensure that the rules of brainstorming are followed (see Chapter 15).
5. The participants run down the list of stakeholders and combine those that are the same but that are stated in different words.
6. The participants identify those stakeholder representatives who should be consulted early on in the initial field study.
7. Finally, the participants identify any 'difficult' people and the stakeholder group they belong to.

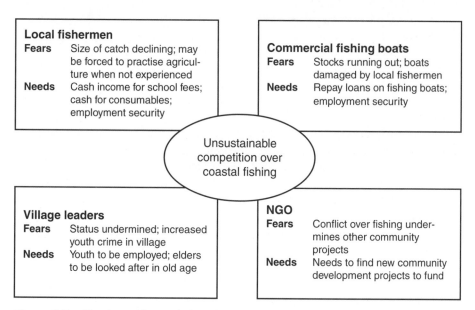

**Figure 6.5.** Needs and fears analysis for a conflict over coastal fish stocks (Fiji Islands)

An understanding of the deeper-seated motivations that drive the different stakeholder groups is of critical importance. It is useful to distinguish between two types of underlying motivations:

o **Underlying needs** Human values and interests, such as income, children's education, family welfare, social status and respect.

o **Underlying fears** Human concerns, such as loss of face or status, threat of violence, loss of land or investments, loss of employment and opportunity.

It is often possible to divide needs and fears into two categories: those common to two or more stakeholder groups, and those specific to only one group (see Chapter 4).

Three examples of an office-based analysis of the needs and fears of conflicting stakeholder groups are provided. Figure 6.5 concerns a conflict between local fishermen and commercial fishing boats over the harvesting of coastal fish stocks in the Fiji Islands.

Figure 6.6 follows on from Table 6.1. It illustrates the potential conflict between an oil palm firm and the conservation objectives of a local NGO in Papua New Guinea.

Table 6.2 is taken from a 'parks and people' project in Bolivia. Here, the information on underlying motivations is put alongside the estimated positions of the stakeholders.

## TRAINING EXERCISE 6.5.   NEEDS AND FEARS

### Objective
To construct a provisional picture of the underlying needs and fears motivating different stakeholder groups.

### Tasks
1.  Instruct the participants to maintain the same groups and to work with the same conflict as in Training Exercise 6.4.
2.  As a group, the participants identify the different stakeholders' immediate demands. Encourage them to write these as quotations, e.g. 'We want to be able to fish whenever we want', or 'We don't want the NGO involved any more'.
3.  The group agrees on what the motivating needs and fears are behind these demands.
4.  The group constructs a diagram (as in Figure 6.5) indicating any common needs and fears.
5.  Discuss the results in plenary.

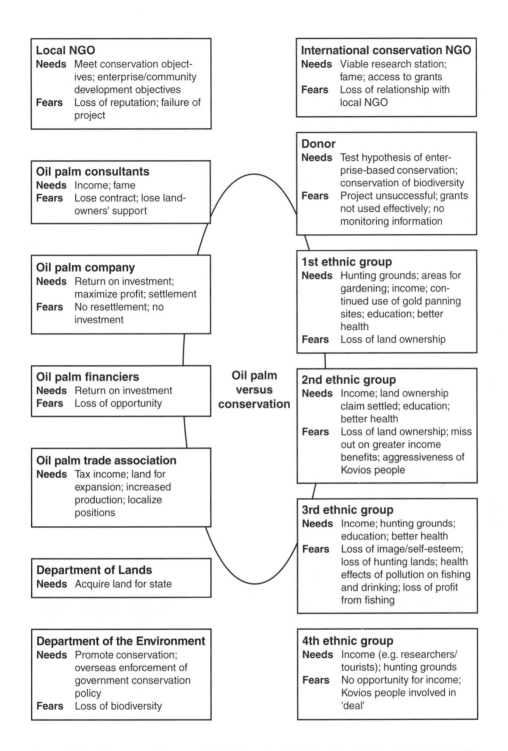

**Local NGO**
**Needs** Meet conservation objectives; enterprise/community
development objectives
**Fears** Loss of reputation; failure of
project

**International conservation NGO**
**Needs** Viable research station;
fame; access to grants
**Fears** Loss of relationship with
local NGO

**Oil palm consultants**
**Needs** Income; fame
**Fears** Lose contract; lose land-
owners' support

**Donor**
**Needs** Test hypothesis of enter-
prise-based conservation;
conservation of biodiversity
**Fears** Project unsuccessful; grants
not used effectively; no
monitoring information

**Oil palm company**
**Needs** Return on investment;
maximize profit; settlement
**Fears** No resettlement; no
investment

**1st ethnic group**
**Needs** Hunting grounds; areas for
gardening; income; con-
tinued use of gold panning
sites; education; better
health
**Fears** Loss of land ownership

**Oil palm financiers**
**Needs** Return on investment
**Fears** Loss of opportunity

**Oil palm
versus
conservation**

**2nd ethnic group**
**Needs** Income; land ownership
claim settled; education;
better health
**Fears** Loss of land ownership; miss
out on greater income
benefits; aggressiveness of
Kovios people

**Oil palm trade association**
**Needs** Tax income; land for
expansion; increased
production; localize
positions

**3rd ethnic group**
**Needs** Income; hunting grounds;
education; better health
**Fears** Loss of image/self-esteem;
loss of hunting lands; health
effects of pollution on fishing
and drinking; loss of profit
from fishing

**Department of Lands**
**Needs** Acquire land for state

**Department of the Environment**
**Needs** Promote conservation;
overseas enforcement of
government conservation
policy
**Fears** Loss of biodiversity

**4th ethnic group**
**Needs** Income (e.g. researchers/
tourists); hunting grounds
**Fears** No opportunity for income;
Kovios people involved in
'deal'

**Figure 6.6.** Needs and fears analysis for a conflict between oil palm and conservation
objectives (Papua New Guinea)

**Table 6.2. Underlying motivations plotted against immediate positions (agroforestry project, Bolivia)**

| Stakeholder group | Positions | Underlying motivations |
|---|---|---|
| **Urban logging interests in town** | ○ Oppose reserve and new forestry legislation<br>○ Ambivalent towards NGO because of its involvement in legal cases against logging companies<br>○ Support indigenous status of reserve | ○ Maintain access to forest resources<br>○ Protect capital investments in logging<br>○ More powerful logging interests mobilize political support from *motersierristas*<br>○ Manipulate indigenous groups inside reserve to grant short-term logging agreements under indigenous arrangements |
| **Municipal authorities** | ○ Favourable<br>○ Desire direct financial support from NGO<br>○ Feel excluded from management of reserve<br>○ Hostile to forestry legislation | ○ Individuals involved in logging<br>○ Seek full logging royalties from Forestry Department<br>○ Fear losing tax revenues from logging inside reserve<br>○ Individuals make private logging agreements inside reserve with indigenous groups |
| ***Corregidores* of local districts** | ○ Favourable | ○ Uphold government policy (represents central government in project area) |
| **Civic Committee of town** | ○ Ambivalent towards NGO<br>○ Considers itself excluded | ○ Maintains status within community<br>○ Protects local resources |
| **Inter-institutional committees of local districts** | ○ Rurrenbaque Institutional Committee (RIC) only recently formed but favourable<br>○ Quiquibey Institutional Committee (QIC) opposed to NGO | ○ RIC strongly promoted by union movement<br>○ QIC strongly influenced by another NGO |
| **Vice-Ministry for Forests, Natural Resources and Environment** | ○ Supports further NGO/reserve separation<br>○ Considers NGO insensitive | ○ Amendments to chainsaw provisions in forestry law 'non-negotiable'<br>○ Avoid political partisanship at local level<br>○ Attract donor funds<br>○ Uphold conservation, biodiversity and public works legislation against indigenous rights to resources in reserve<br>○ Maintain departmental interests |

*(continued)*

**Table 6.2** *(continued)*

| Stakeholder group | Positions | Underlying motivations |
|---|---|---|
| **Conservation Department** | ○ Favourable<br>○ Concerned over need for further separation of NGO and reserve | ○ Awaiting new conservation regulations<br>○ Attract donor funding<br>○ Uphold conservation legislation against indigenous use rights<br>○ Maintain departmental interests |
| **Forest Department** | ○ Favourable<br>○ Desires technical assistance | ○ Enforce new forestry laws on chainsaws<br>○ Retain maximum tax revenues from logging |
| **Vice-Ministry for Indigenous Affairs** | ○ Favours technical support for indigenous administration and reserve management<br>○ Ambivalent to NGO | ○ Uphold indigenous rights to natural resources in reserve<br>○ Demobilization of indigenous groups |

# Chapter 7

# Provisional conflict-management plan

The results of an office-based conflict analysis should be used to prepare a provisional conflict-management plan. This outlines how to manage the conflict.

## Elements of the plan

The provisional plan can include any item needed for consensual negotiations to succeed. Common elements include the following:

*Most practicable strategy*
- o   A combination of one, some or all of the following types of conflict management: force, withdrawal, compromise, accommodation and consensus (see Chapter 4).
- o   The time and resources available, the conflict's urgency and its consequences (see Box 2.4).
- o   The best alternative to negotiated agreement if consensus is not possible.

*Further office-based analysis*
- o   Any further analysis needed.
- o   New research required.

*Participatory conflict analysis*
- o   A way to verify the office-based identification of stakeholder groups and representatives.
- o   A way to verify the office-based analysis of stakeholder groups' underlying motivations.
- o   A programme of initial consultations. This should include how to avoid inflaming the conflict, avoid appearing biased, build rapport to allow discussion of underlying motivations, etc.
- o   A way to explore customary (and institutional and legal) conflict-management mechanisms.

*Capacity building*
o Internal skills training for the co-ordinating agency (NGO, government department, etc.): enhanced skills in personal communication, participatory analysis (e.g. PRA), mediation and facilitation.
o Provisional ideas to build the capacity of conflicting stakeholders. Options include training in personal communication and direct consensual negotiation, and training community leaders or outsiders in third-party facilitation skills.
o Targeting of disenfranchised stakeholders to create a level playing field for the negotiations. This might cover, for example, the use of participatory conflict analysis to build local understanding of the conflict and to clarify underlying motivations.

*Consensual negotiations*
Very provisional ideas for the intended process of consensual negotiation. This may include the following (if appropriate):
o Whether to promote direct (face-to-face) negotiation between the conflicting parties or to use a third-party facilitator.
o Whether this facilitator should be from the community or outside, and whether partial or impartial.
o The timing, duration, location, format and general methods of the negotiations.

## TRAINING EXERCISE 7.1.
## PROVISIONAL CONFLICT-MANAGEMENT PLAN

### Objective
To design a provisional process of analysis, capacity building and consensual negotiation that will guide the consensus building.

### Tasks
1. Keep the participants in the same groups and discussing the same conflict as in Training Exercise 6.5.
2. Ask each group to prepare a provisional conflict-management plan. This should cover the most practicable strategy, further office-based analysis, participatory conflict analysis, capacity building and consensual negotiations.
3. The groups present their plans in plenary.
4. Focus the plenary discussion on the feasibility of the most practicable strategy, whether the approach is likely to be effective (rather than inflaming the conflict), and the importance of flexibility on capacity building and the negotiations.

## *Example 1:* Tourist guesthouse in Papua New Guinea

An example of a provisional conflict-management plan is given in Box 7.1. The example is taken from one of the urgent conflicts identified in the Papua New Guinea project (item 10 in Table 6.1). The conflict concerns the unfair distribution of profit and workload from a tourist guesthouse constructed in a conservation area. The stakeholders are the guesthouse owners, a group of women who cook and clean in the guesthouse, and various community groups jealous at not being included in the enterprise.

The example given is only a provisional plan. The design was to be revised after the field-based participatory conflict analysis was completed.


## *Example 2:* Agroforestry project in Bolivia

This example is taken from an agroforestry project in the buffer zone around the Pilon Lajas Indigenous Peoples/Wildlife Reserve in lowland Bolivia. The project was funded by foreign donors, and was implemented through a local NGO (see also Table 6.2).

Conflicts arose as a result of several factors: competition among NGOs; jealousy between beneficiaries and non-beneficiaries; unmet expectations of beneficiaries; opposition from chainsawyers to the project's work; opposition by a politicized NGO, local logging companies, urban logging interests and indigenous groups to work in the reserve; and encroachment by *campesinos* into indigenous people's land.

The conflict led to an Internet campaign against the project NGO, the occupation of the project outreach headquarters, the detention of project staff, roadblocks, hostility towards project staff and the withdrawal of activities from one-third of the project area.

The conflict analysis included a review of:
o   the underlying causes of the conflict (Box 7.2);
o   stakeholder mapping (Figure 6.4);
o   the identification of the key conflicts and tensions;
o   temporal and spatial conflict mapping;
o   an evaluation of previous attempts to mitigate the conflict; and
o   a participatory assessment of risks of future conflict and the opportunities to mitigate them.

The conflict management plan included:
o   Implementation of an ongoing and accurate project communications strategy aimed at the local level.
o   Postponement of a proposed mass-media communication strategy until the project NGO's involvement in the reserve had been clarified.

## Box 7.1.  Provisional conflict-management plan for tourist guesthouse (Papua New Guinea)

### Most practicable strategy of conflict management

Consensual negotiation, combined with the development of other community-based enterprises. Rather than targeting just the immediate conflicting parties, build the facilitation and negotiation skills of the whole community. Avoid using an outside facilitator if possible.

The cultural diversity of conflicting parties may be too great to build these skills on to traditional approaches. An independent mechanism to manage conflicts is needed.

The best alternative to negotiated agreement is for the co-ordinating NGO to threaten to withdraw.

### Further office-based conflict analysis

To be revisited after the participatory conflict analysis (see below).

### Participatory conflict analysis

o  Verify the range of stakeholder groups and their initial legitimate representatives.
o  Verify the stakeholders' underlying fears and needs.
o  Explore the idea of building the community's facilitation and negotiation skills, and whether this will help manage conflicts.
o  Identify the community's training needs.

The following tools will be used:
o  Focus groups, using wealth ranking to select and stratify samples.
o  Consultation with representative subgroups from each stakeholder group.
o  Informal discussions: consult with a wider range of people than simply the current opinion leaders.
o  Informal discussions followed by more formal meetings based on stakeholder groupings.

### Consensual negotiation (provisional recommendation)

o  Informal discussions to introduce the idea of communities managing their own conflicts through consensual negotiation.
o  Community training in communication skills, direct negotiation, facilitation and mediation.
o  Community groups to manage guesthouse disputes themselves (perhaps with incentive of expanded enterprises).

71

o   Transfer of the NGOs' current programme of assistance for the reserve to the government authorities.
o   Project NGO to sign of letters of intent with the main *campesino*, indigenous and government organizations in the project area.
o   Dispute management training for senior project NGO staff, the reserve authorities and other local leaders.

---

**Box 7.2.  Underlying causes of conflict (Pilon Lajas, Bolivia)**

o  Local colonist unions (ex-miners) whose authority is threatened by new producer associations.
o  A colonist union movement (fuelled by external supporters) capable of mobilizing local support for wider political motives.
o  Resource-poor local government, aligned to the private sector.
o  Under-resourced NGOs, often operating in competition with each other rather than in co-operation.
o  An increasingly politically mobilized indigenous population.
o  A shift towards riskier livelihoods (e.g. use of chainsaws) as a result of new forestry legislation.
o  Uncertainty over land rights and property ownership.

# Chapter 8

# Participatory conflict analysis

## Leaving the situation alone

The office-based conflict analysis can be thought of as the first step in a needs assessment of the situation. One option will be to leave the conflict situation as it is, i.e. to do nothing. There may be at least two reasons for such a decision. The first is that the existing mechanisms to managing conflict (customary, institutional and legal) are effective and can be left to work. The second is that leaving the conflict alone will bring benefits that outweigh any possible negative effects. For example, the conflict may encourage the parties to form a new institution or mechanism that will solve both the immediate conflict and future disputes. Alternatively, the conflict may help to publicize social or political injustices that intervention might perpetuate.

The key question is: do the benefits of managing the conflict outweigh the benefits of leaving things as they are?

## Initial participatory conflict analysis

If the office-based analysis identifies the need for consensual negotiation, the findings of the analysis will need to be tested in the field. At the same time, it is necessary to begin building rapport with the different stakeholder groups.

Think carefully about how to approach the various stakeholders. For example, it may be best to avoid the temptation to rush to speak with the supposed representatives of indigenous community groups. These people may not yet see themselves as leaders, and treating them as such may cause resentment. In any case, the community may nominate someone completely different to speak on its behalf. It is far safer to begin consultation with customary leaders and to work outwards from there.

It is vital to generate enough trust to allow discussions on the conflict with different stakeholders without inflaming the situation.

Box 8.1 lists some of the steps involved in participatory conflict analysis.

---

**Box 8.1.  Basic steps in participatory conflict analysis**

1. Build rapport.
2. Verify the stakeholder groups and group representatives.
3. Verify their underlying motivations, needs and fears.
4. Consult on the most practicable strategy to manage the conflict (this should include doing nothing).
5. Clarify the conflict in terms of geography, timing, quantification, people affected, etc.
6. If consensual negotiation is chosen, explore the relevant existing customary, institutional and legal conflict-management mechanisms.
7. Consult on whether to try to build consensual negotiation on to the existing mechanisms, or to manage the conflict independently from them.
8. Consult on the capacity-building options available to support the negotiations.

---

# Clarification

## Clarifying underlying motivations

Clarification of the underlying motivations driving the stakeholders is one of the principles of consensus building. It is essential to an effective process of consensual negotiation.

The participatory analysis should seek to clarify the deeper needs and fears that motivate individuals and groups. Some questions to do this are given in Chapter 4. These questions will help verify the results of the office-based analysis of needs and fears. Success will depend largely on the rapport and trust built up with the stakeholder groups. Even when a stakeholder's deeper motivations are revealed, more time and rapport may be needed before he or she is willing to have them revealed to other parties.

When to clarify the underlying motivations and reveal them to the other stakeholders is a matter of judgement. It may happen at the same time as the stakeholder groups are verified, after the capacity building or during a workshop.

## Spatial and temporal clarification

It is important for stakeholders to be specific in describing their underlying motivations. People tend to generalize and sometimes exaggerate their motivations, particularly in terms of geography (where something is located), time (when it is needed) and quantities (the cost, amount or volume needed).

74

## TRAINING EXERCISE 8.1.   CLARIFICATION III

### Objective
To develop skills in clarifying the underlying motivations of conflicting parties.

### Tasks
1.  In plenary, ask the participants to collectively identify a past conflict that all know of and which it is safe to discuss as an exercise (for example, an international disagreement or a familiar community project that generated conflict).
2.  Divide the participants into pairs.
3.  Invite half of the pairs to be facilitators.
4.  For the remaining pairs, assign each a role as one of the stakeholders in the conflict (e.g. government ministry, donor agency, community group).
5.  Instruct the facilitating pairs to develop a set of semi-structured questions to unearth the underlying motivations, needs and fears of the stakeholder groups (examples are given in Chapter 4).
6.  Instruct each stakeholder pair to agree on their immediate positions about the conflict and their underlying motivations (goals, values, needs and fears).
7.  Assign each facilitating pair to one of the stakeholder pairs. The facilitating pair spends 30 minutes trying to understand the underlying motivations of the stakeholder pair.
8.  Instruct the facilitating pair to take things slowly, i.e. first build some rapport, but avoid lingering on the stakeholder's immediate positions.
9.  Each pair presents back its findings in plenary.
10. Select one of the facilitation pairs to cluster the common motivations and to isolate the different individual motivations.

In community-based natural resource projects, the where and when of resource use can be critical.

The use of community participation methods has increased dramatically over the past ten years. This is partly because conventional questionnaires fail to allow community members to express what is important to them or to participate fully in local decision making. The range of community participation methods is too numerous to describe in detail here. For details, see Pretty et al. (1995).

Figure 8.1, Figure 8.2 and Table 8.1 show the use of community participation techniques (in this case transect walks, sketch mapping, seasonal calendars and a simplified conflict analysis framework; see Chapter 9) to help reframe a conflict between a logging company and a women's group. The exercises were held separately with each set of stakeholders.

At first, the women's group said they wanted to gather fruit and fuelwood from the whole area east of the main road. They also said that the river needed to be freed of pollution along its entire length. Transect walks and drawing a sketch map with the women revealed the true geographic extent of these needs (Figure 8.1).

Similarly, the logging company first stated that it required logging rights all year round, and that the women should not enter the concession area at any time. Using participatory techniques, a seasonal calendar (Figure 8.2) was compiled independently with each group. This showed that each group needed access at certain times of year but not at others. There was only two months' overlap between the two periods.

Lastly, the women's needs for fuelwood, fruits and drinking water were clarified. This made it possible to describe accurately the harm logging caused to these interests (Table 8.1).

## Clarification in complex situations

If the situation involves many conflicts and complicated interplay between the stakeholder groups, a more systematic approach may be needed. Such complexity commonly exists in large-scale rural livelihood projects, such as the management of coastal zones or protected areas. Chapter 9 describes such an approach – the conflict analysis framework – which combines information from PRA with external stakeholder assessment.

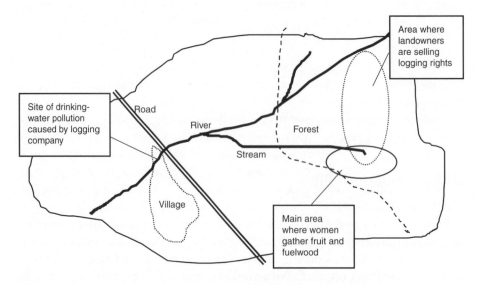

**Figure 8.1.** Example of clarification using a composite map

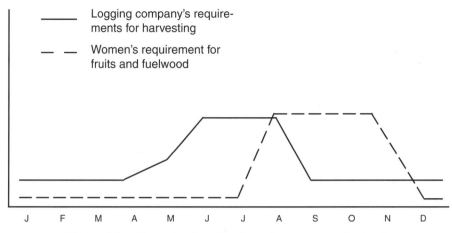

**Figure 8.2.** Example of clarification using a seasonal calendar

Table 8.1. **Example of clarification using a conflict analysis framework**

| Activities affected by conflict | Specific resources affected | Magnitude of conflict[a] | Importance of conflict[b] |
|---|---|---|---|
| **Women's group** | | | |
| Collecting non-timber forest products | Mopane fuelwood | 25% | High |
| | Marula fruit | 50% | Low |
| Collecting drinking water | Village standpipe | 50% | Moderate |
| **Logging company** | etc. | etc. | etc. |

[a] Percentage reduction in resource availability to the stakeholder group.

[b] Importance in sustaining livelihood or protecting human welfare.

## Using community video

Short video films made by the different stakeholders can be a powerful medium to focus attention on the true parameters of the conflict. Community video can also help inform other parties of the community's views, their needs and fears, and their ideas for solutions. It can be a useful medium for clarifying conflicts both among community groups and between local groups and outsiders.

# Building on customary, institutional and legal mechanisms

## Customary mechanisms

Existing customary mechanisms of community leaders and groups can be effective in managing conflicts. These mechanisms are often based on processes of consensus building or arbitration. They primarily target family, labour and civil disputes; environmental disputes are a new and growing area. Examples include the *barangay* justice system in The Philippines; Sri Lanka's village-level mediation panels; the *lok adalats* (people's courts) in the Indian states of Gujarat and Uttar Pradesh; and the *taha* system of the Maoris in New Zealand.

## Overwhelming conflict

The problem with customary management comes when new development pressures stimulate conflicts that overwhelm the mechanisms. The conflicting parties may be creative enough to modify the customary mechanism, or to develop new institutions or mechanisms to deal with these situations. But this is often not possible, at least within the timescale of the project in question. This is where the techniques described in this book can be used.

## Cultural scenarios

How to employ consensus-building techniques to help manage these overwhelming conflicts depends to a large degree on the cultural diversity of the different stakeholder groups involved. Two broad scenarios can be identified:

○ **Cultural uniformity**, where the different stakeholder groups (who may or may not be from different cultures) view conflict and its management in a similar way.

○ **Cultural diversity**, where the different stakeholder groups have different, perhaps mutually incompatible, ways of viewing and managing conflict.

These two scenarios are discussed below (see also Figure 8.3).

## Cultural uniformity

An example of cultural uniformity with regard to conflict is seen among indigenous groups in community forestry projects in Fiji. Here, most community groups share a common view of conflict and how to manage it. Minor disputes over forest management (for example, the distribution of profits within groups of landowners) are usually resolved through customary means, for example through facilitation by the Mataqali head. Where this is ineffective, or where more stakeholders are involved (such as a boundary dispute between two groups of landowners), an institutional resolution may be sought. This might mean intervention by the Native Lands Trust Board or another government agency, or recourse to the legal system.

Some conflicts overwhelm these existing mechanisms. Examples are conflicts over the level of involvement of different landowners in a project, between project participants and non-participants, or over the environmental damage caused by the project.

If cultural diversity is low, consensus-building techniques should try to strengthen the existing mechanisms, starting with customary mechanisms, and moving on to institutional and legal ones where relevant. See Box 10.1 for some ways of doing this.

## Cultural diversity

In contrast to the Fiji case, natural resource projects in Papua New Guinea often work in communities with widely different cultures. Where two or more different ethnic groups are involved in a project, disputes often arise

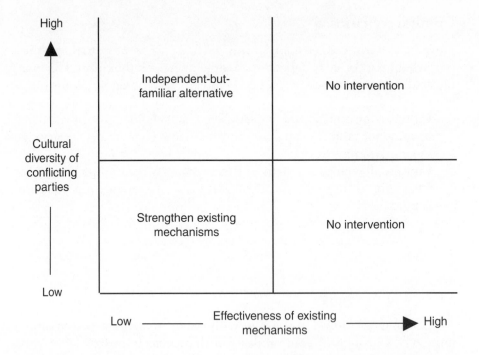

**Figure 8.3.** Consideration of existing mechanisms in managing overwhelming conflicts

over land ownership and the distribution of work or of profits. For example, the conflicting parties often speak different languages, and there are many possible mediators or arbitrators.

Communities are increasingly turning to outside institutions to help resolve their disputes, especially in land-ownership cases. For example, a land mediator may be invited to hear arguments over the historical legitimacy of the various claims. If the mediator is unable to find a resolution, one or more of the parties may request the local court to pass judgement.

But these institutional and legal mechanisms are often too expensive, take too long or are seen as biased. As in the Fiji Islands, development pressures simply overwhelm the existing conflict-settlement mechanisms.

The wide cultural diversity in Papua New Guinea suggests that it may be better to develop some independent system to manage conflicts, rather than to try to strengthen existing mechanisms. As far as possible, the new system should be viewed by all parties as impartial and it should contain elements familiar to each.

For example, the new system might include a third-party impartial facilitator. This is because most ethnic groups in Papua New Guinea rely on a third-party mediator to help settle disputes.

## Modelling customary, institutional and legal mechanisms

If the participatory conflict analysis indicates that existing mechanisms are not likely to resolve the dispute quickly enough, the next step is to explore whether these mechanisms can be strengthened.

Six key components of existing mechanisms can be analysed: the type of negotiation; the status of the facilitator; the meeting format; the process of dialogue; the reaching of agreement; and the participation of uninvolved parties. Table 8.2 shows some of the options for various aspects of these components. It can be used as a form to model the existing mechanisms: just circle the appropriate options in the last column and add comments as required. A new form should be used for each of the stakeholders and the possible mechanisms considered.

Table 8.3 shows the results of such modelling in an NGO-sponsored community-based ecoforestry project in Fiji. The planning for this project

81

**Table 8.2.  Alternative customary conflict-management mechanisms**

| Component | Aspect | Option |
|---|---|---|
| **Type of negotiation** | Direct person-to-person negotiation | ○ Representatives<br>○ All interested parties |
| | Third party facilitation/ mediation | ○ Legal representative<br>○ Government representative<br>○ Respected community members<br>○ Council of elders<br>○ Elected leaders<br>○ Self-imposed leaders<br>○ Hereditary leaders |
| **Preferred status of facilitator(s)** | Impartial | ○ Insider<br>○ Outsider |
| | Partial | ○ Insider<br>○ Outsider |
| **Meeting format** | | ○ Individual negotiations with conflicting parties<br>○ Individual then joint negotiations<br>○ Joint negotiations involving all parties |
| **Process of dialogue** | Eligibility | ○ Prioritized by status<br>○ All eligible |
| | Structure | ○ One person at a time<br>○ Overlapping speakers<br>○ Multiple small discussions |
| | Communication style | ○ Direct and confrontational<br>○ Indirect and non-confrontational (e.g. talking through proposed solutions) |
| **Reaching agreement** | Process | ○ Judgement<br>○ Consensus arbitration panel of peers |
| | Decision format | ○ Oral third-party verification<br>○ Legally binding<br>○ Written (e.g. memorandum of understanding)<br>○ Exchange of gifts |
| | Enforcement | ○ Legal enforcement<br>○ Memorandum of understanding, enforceable under contract law<br>○ Conditional fines and punishments<br>○ Peer social pressure |
| **Participation of parties not involved in the conflict** | | ○ None<br>○ Observers<br>○ Advisers<br>○ Process recorders<br>○ Implementation monitors<br>○ Implementation evaluators |

identified potential disputes between community groups over land ownership boundaries. Customary mechanisms are commonly used to settle such disputes; they are expected to solve some 50 per cent of cases. Institutional mechanisms are called on next; they resolve a further 20 per cent of cases. It is rare for the courts to be involved, so legal mechanisms have been omitted from the analysis. The final column of the table shows possible ways of strengthening the existing mechanisms.

Such an analysis also makes it possible to decide whether to adopt an independent conflict-management system rather than try to strengthen the existing mechanisms.

# Revised conflict-management plan

## Outputs of participatory conflict analysis

The participatory conflict analysis phase of the process should have:
o   built rapport between the conflicting parties and between these parties and the facilitator (if one is to be used)
o   led to agreement on the most practicable strategy for managing the current conflict, and perhaps future conflicts too
o   clarified the key stakeholder groups and their representatives
o   clarified and provided details about the stakeholders' underlying motivations
o   determined whether to strengthen the existing conflict-management mechanisms or to develop an independent system
o   identified the available options for capacity building.

The provisional conflict-management plan can now be revised in this light. In particular, it should now be possible to plan a programme of capacity building and to develop detailed plans for consensual negotiations.

## Actual versus potential conflicts

There are some key differences in the way office-based and participatory conflict analysis is undertaken for actual conflicts afflicting projects midstream, as against those that are predicted during a project's planning phase.

Live conflicts are prioritized mainly in the office, rather than through participatory analysis. This exercise aims to single out urgent and significant conflicts, and those that trigger other disputes. A detailed analysis of the stakeholders, and of any common ground they share, helps determine how

**Table 8.3.** Example of modelling existing conflict-management mechanisms (boundary dispute, Fiji)

| Key components of existing mechanisms | Customary mechanism | Institutional mechanism | Suggested strengthening of existing mechanisms |
|---|---|---|---|
| **Type of negotiation** | Direct, person-to-person negotiations between Mataqali heads | Third-party facilitation by provincial commissioner for Native Land Trust Board (NLTB) | No intervention |
| **Perceived status of facilitator** | No facilitation | Outside, impartial | No intervention |
| **Meeting format** | Consultation of landowners followed by joint meeting of Mataqali heads | Consultation of landowners followed by joint meeting of Mataqali heads, chaired by NLTB commissioner | No intervention |
| **Process of dialogue** | All eligible; one person at a time; non-confrontational | All eligible; one person at a time; non-confrontational | Train Mataqali heads and provincial commissioner in facilitation skills |
| **Reaching agreement** | By consensus; verbally binding; no enforcement | By judgement against pre-existing maps; legally binding and enforceable under law | Deposit existing maps with area chief and ensure Mataqali heads understand them |
| **Participation of parties not involved in the conflict** | Area chief as observer and adviser | Area chief as observer and adviser | Add NGO project-sponsor as observer |

to begin dialogue. The modelling exercise during participatory analysis can help reveal whether strengthening existing mechanisms might be effective in managing the conflict.

Participatory analysis plays a larger role in preparing for potential conflicts. The office-based analysis first identifies who might evaluate existing conflict-management mechanisms. The participatory analysis then identifies which disputes these mechanisms are unlikely to resolve, how to strengthen the existing mechanisms and what new independent process might be needed. A detailed stakeholder analysis is necessary only for conflicts that are unlikely to be managed by the existing mechanisms.

# Chapter 9

# The conflict analysis framework

This chapter outlines the conflict analysis framework – a technique that helps link PRA to policy. This approach is useful for systematic clarification of complex conflicts.

The technique was developed to facilitate community involvement in formulating resource policies and management plans for Game Management Areas across Zambia – areas that support natural resources important to both wildlife conservation and the livelihoods of local people. It was piloted with communities in two areas in Zambia in December 1995. It was implemented together with of the World Wide Fund for Nature (WWF) Zambia Country Office, the WWF Bangweulu Wetlands Project in northeast Zambia, and the Zambian National Parks and Wildlife Service.

In attempts to link participatory analysis with policy formulation, three problems stand out:

o  Local values and perceptions may be distorted when PRA facilitators interpret the information for policymakers.
o  Participating communities often do not benefit from a PRA exercise. PRA may extract information rather than benefit local people directly by solving their problems or empowering them.
o  It is difficult – logistically, culturally and politically – to bring local people around the policy formulation table.

A means is therefore needed to represent the views of local people when formulating policy and to provide immediate, tangible benefits to community participants. The conflict analysis framework tries to do this.

## Goal of the conflict analysis framework

The conflict analysis framework provides a systematic, participatory analysis of the use of resources by local people. The ideas behind the analysis, and the design of the summary matrix, are drawn from conflict resolution and environmental impact assessment.

The tool was developed to aid sustainable resource management in protected areas. It summarizes the conflicts that local people perceive between their use of natural resources (wildlife, fish, water, timber, fertile land, fuelwood, etc.) and the interests of other stakeholders (e.g. government conservation authorities, tourist and safari operators, forestry and water resource departments, district council, etc.).

While it was developed for use in protected areas, the tool could help link PRA to policy formulation wherever the policy aims to address conflicts over finite resources. Thus it might also be useful in determining policies for infrastructure (e.g. transport, electricity) or access to education and health services.

Table 9.1 shows an extract from one of the summary matrices generated in the Zambia pilot studies. Table 9.2 is an example of an exploded row from this table; it shows the importance of providing a full, and where possible quantified, explanation of the conflict or concern.

The first column in Table 9.1 summarizes the principal livelihood activities of local people. The second column shows those natural resources important to each activity. PRA techniques useful in completing this analysis include historical profiles, time trends, transects, village resource maps, institutional Venn diagrams, and daily routine and seasonal calendars. Information about the timing, location and users of resources is recorded separately during the PRA exercise.

The PRA fieldwork is preceded by a separate, institutional stakeholder assessment of the conservation, economic and political forces acting on the local resource base (Warner, 1995). This external assessment is then brought alongside the internal assessment generated through the PRA. Issues identified by the external stakeholders are entered into the appropriate rows in the third column of the table.

## Conflicts and concerns

Conflict resolution emphasizes the need to find common ground among stakeholders. Thus, the fourth column shows not only community-perceived conflicts, but also 'concerns'. These are resource issues that local people think are important, but which do not cause direct conflict with external stakeholders. Examples might include contaminated drinking water or local labour shortages.

Analysing concerns provides the policy formulation process with additional options, introducing additional bargaining chips to the policy formulation process.

For example, a programme might be started to dig wells if local people agree to stop hunting wildlife. However, experience has shown that such unrelated arrangements are invariably unsustainable. It is better for programmes to be clearly associated with the proposed policy, such as an organization that protects wildlife by sharing profits from safari hunting with would-be poachers (e.g. the Zimbabwe CAMPFIRE programme).

Table 9.1. Extract from a summary matrix[a]

| Community activities | Community resources | Conservation conflicts | Community-perceived conflicts/concerns | Primary resource stakeholders | | | | | |
| | | | | Men | | | Women | | |
| | | | | Magnitude | Resolution | Importance | Magnitude | Resolution | Importance |
|---|---|---|---|---|---|---|---|---|---|
| **Shifting cultivation** | Land with adequate regrowth | Elephant habitat loss | Distance/time | 25% | Prohibitive | Medium | 25% | Prohibitive | Medium |
| | Logs for charcoal | Elephant habitat loss | Loss of regenerative potential of forest | 50% | Prohibitive | High | 50% | Prohibitive | High |
| | Cassava crop | Elephant habitat loss | Crop damage (elephants) | 40% | External | Low | 40% | External | Low |
| **Fishing** | Fish stocks | Loss of food sources for endangered bird species | Progressively reduced catches & size of fish | 50% | Internal | Medium | 50% | Internal | Medium |
| **Hunting**[b] | Buffalo and other game species | Declining game populations | Hunting restrictions | 80% | External | Medium | – | – | – |
| **Firewood collection** | Time, labour | Biodiversity and elephant habitat loss | Not available during wet season | – | – | – | 50% | External | High |
| **Permanent agriculture**[c] | Fertilizer | | Late delivery (1 month) | 40% | External | High | – | – | – |

a   Result of a conflict analysis in two Game Management Areas in Zambia.
b   See Table 9.3
c   See Table 9.2.

## Prioritizing

The final columns of Table 9.1 prioritize the community's resource conflicts and concerns. Drawing on environmental impact assessment, each conflict or concern is divided into its 'magnitude' and 'importance'.

### Magnitude

The magnitude of the conflict is given as a percentage. The major users of the resource are asked to say what proportion of a resource or service is lost or absent as a result of the conflict. For example, if on average farmers lose 50 per cent of their maize crops to trampling by wildlife each year, then the magnitude of the conflict is 50 per cent.

If there is no direct conflict, but instead the community perceives a development concern (such as poor firewood supplies in the wet season), the magnitude of the problem can still be measured in percentage terms. For example, taking the dry season fuelwood supply as the norm, people who regularly collect firewood might estimate that only two-thirds of domestic fuel needs are met in the wet season. The magnitude of this concern would be 33 per cent. A full explanation of the seasonality and nature of the concern would also be documented (this is shown in Table 9.2).

**Table 9.2. Supporting documentation for bottom row of Table 9.1**

| Community activity | Community resource | Conflict/resolution |
|---|---|---|
| Permanent agriculture | **Fertilizer:** According to village elders, in the mid-1960s, cheap synthetic fertilizers were introduced to aid maize cultivation. This led to a switch away from organic (grasses and manure) fertilizers, resulting in a growing dependency on synthetics | **Magnitude:** Landholders depend on the delivery of fertilizers by outside agencies. Over the past few years the village's low status has meant that fertilizers arrive late (average delay = 1 month). Yields and incomes have declined: participants suggested that the late fertilizer deliveries cut maize yields by 40%, more than wiping out their profits. In addition, fertilizer costs have risen steadily, forcing an increasing number of villagers into debt (**40%**) |
| | | **Importance:** Maize is the primary source of cash income, so the late arrival and rising price of fertilizers is of critical importance. Because maize production (and to a certain extent household income expenditure) is the preserve of village men, women and waged labourers saw this concern as less critical. The women are more concerned with food security, and so with cassava (**high**) |
| | | **Resolution:** It would be difficult to return to organic fertilization because 3–4 years' transition would be needed to rebuild natural soil fertility. However, such a return would remove dependency and the debt burden of villagers who now rely on imported fertilizers (**external**) |

The percentage figures indicate the scale of the conflict or concern. To arrive at these figures, it is necessary to explore the impact of the problem on the people it affects. The single figure is a clear, simple way of making outsiders aware of how conflicts over resources affect the community.

Different groups of local people use different natural resources. For ease of interpretation, however, the summary matrix gives only the main community stakeholders – those directly dependent on a particular resource in terms of employment, gender, wealth, etc. Other cases may require different divisions or levels of disaggregation.

### Importance

The magnitude of a conflict or concern does not necessarily reflect its significance to livelihood security or welfare of the major stakeholders. For example, if elephants trample a cassava crop during the hungry season (before maize is ready for harvest), the effect may be devastating, even though the crop loss, in terms of annual yield, is relatively small.

The importance of a conflict or concern is measured on a three-point scale: high, medium or low.

These definitions are intentionally open-ended. The primary stakeholders (or the community as a whole) can determine the criteria for importance. PRA techniques useful for prioritizing conflicts and gauging importance include pair-wise comparisons, direct matrix ranking and cluster ranking.

As with the magnitude figures, the importance classifications are indicative only. Supporting documentation, shown in Table 9.2, is given for each classification. This details the types of resource affected, their location, when they are collected or used, issues of uncertainty and risk, and the rationale behind the magnitude and importance classifications.

## Resolutions

The conflict analysis framework is not a tool for policy formulation itself. Rather, it is a means to bring the community perspective into a wider process of building consensus among all stakeholders who are likely to be affected by, or influential in, the policy. It can also be used to encourage local people to investigate options for resolving their perceived resource conflicts. These options can then be used as starting points for wider negotiations over policy.

Conflict resolutions are divided into three types:
o  Those that can be implemented **internally** to the affected stakeholder group and which are readily available, affordable and socially acceptable.
o  Those requiring **external** financial or technical assistance.
o  Those that are **prohibitive** due to financial, social or environmental costs.

# Community action proposals

The conflict analysis framework supports the development of community action proposals. These provide an incentive for local people to participate in policy formulation. They also build trust between communities and the external stakeholders. Community action proposals are project or action outlines that seek to bring rapid, tangible benefits to the participating communities. They are intended for implementation without the need for wider stakeholder agreement, or for substantial financial or technical assistance.

Community action proposals address the problem of policy-based PRAs raising false short-term expectations by limiting themselves to information extraction. Table 9.3 is an example of a proposal that relates to the hunting restrictions identified in Table 9.1.

**Table 9.3. Example of a community action proposal**

**Buffalo habitat enhancement scheme**

| | |
|---|---|
| What | The granting, by the Ministry of Tourism, of a special licence for the community to hunt buffalo (quota of 50 per year) within the local area in return for enhancing buffalo wildlife habitats through forage planting and refraining from further forest encroachment |
| Why | In medium term (3–5 years), the proposal will increase population of buffalo in the protected area as well as enhancing habitats for other species |
| Who implements | Village Wildlife Management Sub-Authority to co-ordinate team of conservation workers from the community |
| Who benefits | All households who consume bush meat, and in the longer term, the whole village through increased safari-hunting revenues redistributed to communities |
| Where | Forest encroachment halted to south of village in areas of buffalo and other wildlife migration routes. Also forage planting along migration routes and along river banks where buffalo and other wildlife congregate during the dry season |
| When | Maximum efforts to prevent forest encroachment targeted in October/November. Forage planting concentrated in December to deliver habitat and food refuges in the dry season |
| How | Village conservation teams to be provided with seeds and tools for forage planting, and village scouts hired in October/November to monitor for forest encroachment |
| Cost | US$ 10 000 per year |
| Time to benefits | 1. Special licence for village buffalo quota delivers bush meat to village (for consumption or sale) within six months of application |
| | 2. Increase in buffalo and other wildlife populations from habitat improvements expected to give rise to increase in safari hunting revenues in years 3–5 |
| | 3. Payment of village scouts in October/November provides benefits to certain villagers |

# The Zambian context

It was not the explicit intention of the conflict analysis framework described here to influence policy formulation (although the results are currently being used to support funding applications for future community/wildlife programmes). The conflict analysis framework was piloted:

o   To test the concept of a framework methodology for linking PRA to policy formulation in the field of parks and people.
o   To determine the range of appropriate PRA techniques for this purpose.
o   To expose the Zambian National Parks and Wildlife Service and WWF to the possibility of acting as facilitators to resolve conflicts between local livelihoods and conservation.

The findings of the pilot studies were distributed to the participating communities, the Parks and Wildlife Service, and WWF. The report was also sent to all relevant development agencies (e.g. district council, forestry and agriculture departments, USAID, other NGOs) that might wish to review their regional policies or support the resolutions forwarded by the communities.

# Lessons

Before the conflict analysis framework is applied, screening criteria should be used to determine its feasibility. Most of these criteria would apply to all uses of PRA for policy formulation. They include:

o   The PRA facilitators have sufficient skill and experience.
o   The results of the PRA are fed rapidly into policy formulation through a pre-arranged process.
o   There is a political willingness for policy to be influenced by the local level.
o   External stakeholders are able to negotiate collaboratively.
o   There are adequate human and financial resources for the community action plans to be implemented.

The facilitators may be the conservation authorities. If antagonism with local people is too great, other facilitators, whom local people view as independent, may also be used. If possible, the facilitation team should include the conservation authorities to raise awareness and build trust.

The conflict analysis framework highlights the debate over how far PRA should exclusively promote local knowledge, and how far it should encourage the transfer of outsiders' knowledge to local people. When the resource conflicts perceived by outsiders are introduced to the community, care is needed to avoid biasing the presentation of local views.

The matrix (Table 9.1) is intended to be simple, yet meaningful. To achieve this, a trade-off is needed between detail (disaggregating each community into all stakeholder groups) and simplicity (limiting the disaggregation to the major social divisions, e.g. gender, wealth, education).

A more systematic approach to PRA (by drawing on conflict resolution and environmental impact assessment) improves the quality of the information generated. The conflict analysis framework makes explicit the relative importance of different conflicts.

It is important that both the summary matrix and the background documentation faithfully represent local views.

# Chapter 10

# Capacity building

Capacity building is a key element in conflict management in general, and in consensus building in particular. Many disputes remain unresolved because the mechanisms to resolve them are inadequate, or because the conflicting groups do not have the skills needed to negotiate effectively. Disenfranchized groups (women, youths, minorities, landless people, lower castes) are particularly at a disadvantage.

Some type of capacity building will be needed whether it is decided to construct a new, independent system of conflict management, or to build on existing mechanisms. Various capacity-building options are available, as shown in Boxes 10.1 and 10.2.

---

### Box 10.1. Strengthening existing conflict-management mechanisms

#### Customary mechanisms

○ Provide training in personal communication and consensual negotiation skills to those community groups involved in customary conflict-management mechanisms.
○ Train community leaders in mediation and facilitation skills.

#### Institutional mechanisms

○ Train staff of outside agencies in mediation and facilitation skills.

#### Legal mechanisms

○ Train legal representatives (e.g. local land mediators) in skills for mediating and facilitating win–win settlements (thereby avoiding court proceedings).
○ Train legal representatives (e.g. local magistrates) in interpreting court decisions into win–win judgements.

Certain types of capacity building will occur as an integral part of the participatory conflict analysis. For example, the exercise of clarifying stakeholders' underlying motivations helps develop participants' skills in logical thinking, verbal expression and empathizing; brainstorming develops their creativity and lateral thinking abilities.

Note that all formal capacity building should have been completed before the consensual negotiations themselves begin.

If the conflict is within the community, consider first the possibility of strengthening the negotiation skills of the parties involved. If this is unlikely to be effective, consider next training community leaders in basic third-party facilitated negotiation skills. Only if this is also likely to fail should an outsider be brought in to act as a facilitator. It may be necessary to train the facilitator in consensual negotiation skills.

If outsiders are involved in the dispute, consider first the possibility of training community leaders in consensual negotiation so they can negotiate directly with the outsiders. If this appears unpromising, consider bringing in an outside agency as a facilitator.

---

### Box 10.2 Building an independent mechanism for managing conflict

o Train community groups (or their representatives) for direct face-to-face consensual negotiations. Include both personal communication and negotiation skills.
o Train the most independent community leaders in mediation and facilitation skills.
o Train outside agencies in mediation and facilitation skills so they can offer these services as required.
o Combine elements of existing customary or institutional mechanisms into a new approach to community-based conflict management.

---

# Chapter 11

# Consensual negotiation

Consensual negotiations should begin only when the preparatory conflict analysis, the consensus-building plan and capacity building are as complete as practicable (Figure 5.1). The negotiations themselves will involve the following broad activities. (Some of these may have already been done during the participatory conflict analysis.)

- o   Each stakeholder group develops an understanding of the other groups' underlying motivations.
- o   They generate the widest possible range of options for satisfying these motivations.
- o   The options are prioritized and combined to ensure that all parties gain.
- o   The parties reach consensus over the final agreement.
- o   All are satisfied that implementing the agreement is feasible.

The overall process that binds these activities can vary. Box 11.1 shows some common processes used in consensual negotiation.

## Direct negotiations

Consensus building does not require a third-party facilitator and it is not necessary for all parties to understand the principles of consensual negotiation. If only one of the parties understands these principles, it may be possible for that group to guide a process that explores underlying motivations, widens the options and delivers a win–win outcome. Training Exercises 4.6 and 4.7 can be used to demonstrate this one-track approach.

Direct consensual negotiations can take place among different groups: among groups within the community, between project beneficiaries and other communities, and with government, non-governmental and private organizations.

These negotiations may involve all the individuals in a stakeholder group, or representatives of each group.

---

**Box 11.1. Common processes of consensual negotiation**

### Direct face-to-face negotiation

No facilitator. One or more of the conflicting groups understands the principles and practices of consensus building, and has undertaken the necessary conflict analysis.

### Partial facilitation (brokering)

One of the stakeholders facilitates negotiations between itself and the other parties. This facilitator may be seen as partial to one cause or another, but nevertheless is acceptable (for example, because he or she holds the power to withdraw project funding). Options for managing the process include:

o **Rotational, one-on-one facilitation**: the facilitator negotiates with each stakeholder group or representative in turn.
o **Workshop**: all stakeholder representatives negotiate together under guidance of the facilitator.
o Some combination of the above options.

### Impartial third-party facilitator

The stakeholders agree to allow a third party to facilitate negotiations. The facilitator is seen as impartial and may be known to the parties (an insider) or not known (an outsider). The same options for managing the process apply as above.

---

## Facilitated negotiations

In the developed world, consensual negotiations often include an impartial outsider as facilitator and a workshop bringing together representatives of the stakeholder groups so they can negotiate. However, this model is not necessarily feasible in disputes over natural resources in developing countries: the stakeholders may speak different languages, distrust outsiders and remember a legacy of imposed interventions. Someone familiar to the parties may be needed as facilitator. If such constraints exist, they should become clear during the participatory conflict analysis.

As with direct consensual negotiations, third-party facilitation can take place both among community groups and with outsiders, and can involve everyone in the stakeholder group or just their representatives.

Facilitation may involve meetings with all stakeholder groups (or their representatives) together, or with just one group at a time. A combination of these approaches is likely.

*non-unionised*

Lastly, as indicated in Box 11.1, facilitation does not always have to be by a third party. The conflicting groups might accept a member of one of the conflicting parties as the broker (for example, if he or she has demonstrated understanding of others' concerns and an ability to stay neutral). This internal, impartial, mediator model is rare in many Western nations, where many groups in society understand and readily accept the idea of an unknown professional mediator. It may, however, be acceptable in cultures where 'outsiders' are held in suspicion. A possible solution is to have different types of facilitators or mediators active at different stages in the conflict-resolution process. For example, an impartial outsider (such as an NGO or government agency) could be asked to undertake the participatory conflict analysis or one of the conflicting parties (such as the project sponsor) could take on the role of broker to guide a consensual-negotiation workshop.

## Process of consensual negotiation

The process of consensual negotiation, whether direct or facilitated, can be crudely divided into four key phases: building trust, finding common underlying motivations and interests, widening and prioritizing options, and reaching agreement.

---

**TRAINING EXERCISE 11.1.**
**FACILITATED CONSENSUAL NEGOTIATION:**
**TWO-DAY SIMULATION EXERCISE**

Over a two-day period, the participants must design and implement a process of consensual negotiation that uses the approaches described in this book. The process should take the participants through the phases of: (a) finding common interests; (b) widening and prioritizing options; and (c) reaching agreement. Before starting the simulation, participants should have read all of Chapter 11 to Chapter 15. Allow two full days for this exercise.

### Objective

To develop workshop skills in facilitation and mediation, and to practise bringing conflicting parties to a consensus.

### Tasks

1. Choose one of the following simulation exercises: Coralbay Coastal Resource Management Project (Appendix 3) or Tukubu Conservation Area (Appendix 4).

*(continued)*

## TRAINING EXERCISE 11.1 *(continued)*

2. Give all participants a copy of the general briefing notes.
3. Give each participant the individual briefing notes for one of the stakeholders. They are not permitted to see each others' briefs. If there are too many participants, have pairs of participants play a single role.
4. Explain that the exercise will be broken down into a series of sessions.
5. Explain the aims of the first session (building trust) and the tools to be used. You can choose to use one or more of the following tools: warm up, agenda building and ground rules (see Chapter 15).
6. Out of role, divide the participants into pairs and ask each pair to design the sessions as would-be facilitators. Each pair should design how the session will be played out, whether to work in plenary or small groups, how to adapt the tool to the situation, who will be the intervener and who the recorder, and whether these facilitation roles will be swapped around. Allow around 20 minutes for this design phase.
7. After the 20-minute design phase, select one pair to facilitate the whole session. All other participants play out their roles – NGO, company representatives, etc.
8. At the end of the session, all participants come out of role. In plenary, the trainer draws out the lessons from the session, starting with what the facilitators did well, followed by what they could have done better.
9. In the next session, repeat tasks 6 to 8 above in order to reveal the participants' underlying motivations. The relevant tools are the issue map and strategic questioning (Chapter 15).
10. In the third session, repeat tasks 4 to 8 above, so participants widen and prioritize the options available. For this, the relevant tools are brainstorming, carousel, SWOT analysis, ends–means analysis and prioritizing options (Chapter 15).
11. In session four, again repeat tasks 6 to 8, this time aiming to reach agreement among the stakeholders. The relevant tools are analysis of uncertainty, common grounding matrix, reality testing, setting objectively verifiable indicators and commitment package (also in Chapter 15).
12. Periodically throughout the two days, the participants should be encouraged to mingle with each other within their roles (e.g. over coffee) in order to share each other's underlying motivations, needs and fears. This will help recreate the level of knowledge that the characters would have had as a result of earlier participatory analysis.
13. At the end of the two days, review the exercise in plenary. What did the participants learn, and how might this be useful to them?

## Building trust

By definition, parties entering into a negotiation to resolve conflict are inherently distrustful of each other. Most workshops and meetings will begin with exercises to restore the trust and confidence needed to reach agreement. Various tools can assist in this task. Each has two purposes:
o   To meet the objectives behind the tool, e.g. to build familiarity between parties, set ground rules or develop a shared vision.
o   To improve communications and reach an early consensus between parties around a non-contentious issue.

   Tools to build trust include warm up, agenda building, and ground rules. These are described in Chapter 15.


## Revealing underlying motivations

Much of the analysis of a conflict should have already been done before negotiations start. The second phase of the negotiations will therefore be to take this analysis forward, to assist in revealing the parties' motivations that lie behind the conflict.
   The aim is to begin to find points of common interest between the parties. This could include common underlying motivations, a common understanding of the conflict dynamics or common perceptions of the future (for example the dangers of the conflict escalating).
   Two of the facilitation tools that can be used to build towards common interests are issue map and strategic questioning. These tools are discussed in Chapter 15.


## Widening and prioritizing options

The third phase of consensual negotiations involves identifying the widest possible range of options, and then narrowing these down to those that are most promising. The approach is based on the following assumptions:
o   The different parties have entrenched demands and objectives, encouraging them to look only at a very narrow set of options.
o   Together, the stakeholder groups possess a great deal of creativity, which can be unleashed to transform a conflict into a positive force for change.
o   Different parties have certain underlying motivations in common.
o   It is possible to find solutions to each party's individual underlying motivations that do not impinge on those of others.

Chapter 15 describes some tools that can be used to develop a range of options and then select the most promising ones. These include brainstorming, carousel, SWOT analysis, ends–means analysis, and various tools for prioritizing options.

## Reaching agreement

The fourth phase is where the facilitator's skill is most critical. It entails bringing the most promising options together into an agreement that delivers a win–win outcome. To be accepted by each party, this final agreement may need to encompass a wide range of amendments and conditions.

Part of this phase is the identification and management of uncertainties over the options. These might include a lack of data, the risk of side effects and assumptions about the level of benefits. Scientific and economic studies may be required to reduce these uncertainties and to verify the assumptions. Such studies may include an evaluation of different options or of scenarios within one option (e.g. sensitivity analysis); clarifying the location, timing, quantity and quality of certain options; and exploring the technical, economic, social or environmental feasibility of new ideas.

Benefit/cost analysis might be employed at this stage to calculate who would gain and who would lose from a particular option. For the losers, a way will be needed to transform the option into a win–win outcome: for example, compensation that satisfies their underlying motivations.

When the uncertainties and assumptions are dealt with, the promising options are brought together into an overall agreement. The agreement itself may include requirements for further testing of options, reducing uncertainties and proving assumptions, with particular decisions linked to particular outcomes.

The agreement must be feasible technically, politically and economically: it must be 'reality tested'. The roles, responsibilities and monitoring arrangements must also be decided on.

The final stage is to seek commitment from the members of all the stakeholder groups. For prolonged consensual negotiations, such commitments may need to be sought on a continuous basis. Consensus building that lacks support from people not directly involved in the negotiations must be avoided.

Common tools used in this phase include analysis of uncertainty, common grounding matrix, reality testing, setting objectively verifiable indicators, and commitment package. These are also discussed in Chapter 15.

# Chapter 12

## Facilitation

Disputes over access to natural resources and other assets rarely involve only two groups of people. As the number of stakeholders increases, it is more difficult to manage the dispute through direct face-to-face negotiations. Conflicts involving many stakeholders are likely to require some sort of facilitator or broker.

The power of a facilitator is great. He or she controls the flow and pace of questions brought before the group, sets the tone for discussions, and helps the group focus on important items and get the work done.

To establish authority, the facilitator should:

o   introduce him- or herself and explain how he or she came to be in this role
o   define the functions of the facilitator and the roles of other individuals or groups, e.g. recorder, monitor, 'base groups' (see Chapter 13) and working groups
o   define and review the agenda and work plan for the negotiations
o   review priorities and develop the ground rules for facilitating the workshop.

## Functions of a facilitator

A facilitator performs several different functions in a negotiation: intervener, designer, recorder and supporter (the following is adapted from IUCN, 1995).

### Intervener

This is the function most usually associated with a facilitator. It involves guiding the process by encouraging the participants to work. Specific activities include:

o   directing questions to people who will move the process forward
o   providing a role model for good listening and clarifying
o   reflecting difficult questions back to the participants
o   relating what they say to their underlying motivations
o   watching out for distorted information and meaningless generalizations.

## Designer

This is the function of planning each session and preparing ideas and materials. It may involve presenting the information generated during the previous session: for example, clustering options or presenting draft agreements more coherently. It requires attention to the pace of the process, the participants' dynamics, the time available, the objectives to be met and the tools to be used.

## Recorder

This involves documenting the discussions and making them known: meetings with individuals, the outputs of small groups and the results of multi-stakeholder workshops. Recording is usually done during the sessions themselves. As far as possible, the way the information is recorded should be consistent with the intention, language and words of the participants, so they feel they own what is being summarized.

## Supporter

This function includes: informing people of the arrangements for each session, making sure everybody can attend, translating (or organizing translators), organizing arrangements for the venue, arranging catering and transport, registering participants and writing up any reports required.

The functions of the facilitator can change over the course of the negotiation. For example, in a lengthy workshop with two facilitators, the functions of intervener and recorder may alternate between the two people.

## Ethics of facilitation

The following guidelines are adapted from IUCN (1995).
o   Explain what you are doing at each stage.
o   Demystify the techniques you use.
o   Keep your ego out of the process, so that the participants can develop their own dialogue and agreement.
o   Facilitate, don't manipulate.
o   Never ask someone to repeat or give details of their demands and immediate positions. Instead, ask why they have these demands and so develop an understanding of their underlying motivations. (However,

some facilitators consider asking 'why' to be a sign of immaturity. They would argue that soliciting underlying motivations is more subtle and protracted, involving much story-telling and dependent on a high degree of trust and rapport.)

o  Avoid becoming an advocate for any particular outcome.

o  Avoid becoming an ally of any individual or subgroup.

o  Avoid the temptation to become a psychotherapist: you have no authority to give individuals advice or guidance.

o  If it becomes apparent that you have a view (i.e. that you become partial rather than impartial), ask the group to judge if you should continue in your role, and if so, how to manage this change.

o  Avoid jargon, technical terms and references that provoke surprise or disagreement.

o  Help the participants to slow down so as to avoid facilitating infeasible and unworkable agreements. Control the pace of the process. Don't rush to an agreement.

o  Learn to recognize when some degree of fudging is essential if there is to be progress. For example, an agreement may need to incorporate a requirement for additional studies that show a particular expectation is valid.

# Chapter 13

# Workshop design and methods

Workshops are common both in consensual negotiation and in training to build stakeholders' capacity. Workshops may be held with members of a single stakeholder group, or many different stakeholders may be present, for example in order to reach an agreement. To ensure success, the right design and methods are important. Different designs will be needed if the aim is to develop common interests, widen options or reach agreement, or if all three phases are covered in one workshop.

## Basics of workshop design

*Which stakeholder groups?*   In the early stages of conflict management, separate workshops are often held with each conflicting party. The facilitator meets with each party in turn. The facilitator's role is to make sure that all parties understand their own and each other's perceptions of the conflict. These workshops can be part of the participatory conflict analysis.

Such 'shuttle' workshops should build a core of agreement among the parties about what can be negotiated. Any shared perceptions, underlying motivations, needs and values must be made explicit. The parties should agree how the process is to be managed, including the broad workshop methods likely to be employed. They should also agree what will happen when the conflicting parties first meet.

When the level of mutual understanding enables the sides to meet without violence, workshops can involve several or all of the stakeholder groups.

*One-off or a series?*   A workshop may be a one-off activity, lasting a few hours; it may be part of a series of workshops with the same participants (or with different ones); or it may last several days, weeks or months.

*Objective*   The workshop objective should be clear. For example, is it to introduce ideas of conflict escalation and management, to seek common interests among stakeholders or to review the implementation of agreements?

*Participants*   Should the workshop participants be chosen by the stakeholder group or selected and invited by a third party?

*Keeping non-participants informed* How will the representatives at the workshop keep their group informed of what is happening and make sure they support it? For example, should the wider group be able to vote on options developed at the workshop? Or could observers from each group attend the workshop to monitor and report back to the group?

*Group management* For larger and longer processes of conflict management, it may be necessary to form subgroups for specific purposes. Subgroups might include the following:

o **Core group** This is a group of key stakeholder representatives with whom the overall process of consensual negotiation is conducted. These parties then refer back to their constituents.
o **Base groups** These are smaller groups within the core group, which meet regularly within the workshop setting and which provide an opportunity for participants to share and discuss their thoughts and feelings privately.
o **Working groups** These are charged with looking at particular issues, such as the technical verification of different options. Working groups may be permanent or temporary.
o **Steering committee** This oversees changes in the negotiation process and tracks progress.
o **Decision-making forum** This may or may not be the same as the core group.
o **Implementation group** This verifies that agreements are implemented and adhered to.

*Facilitator* Considerations should include who is available to facilitate the workshop, how they are perceived by the participants (e.g. their class, religion, gender, status as outsiders or insiders, appropriateness), the workshop location and the different cultural characteristics of the stakeholder groups.

*Location and timing* Where, when and for how long will the workshop be held? The location and timing must be chosen so that people will be able to attend. The setting must be conducive to collaborative negotiation. For example, a workshop facilitated by an outsider within a village, in full view of the villagers, might give the impression that the community leaders' authority is being undermined.

*Language* Translation slows things down and changes the workshop dynamics, but this can sometimes be turned into a positive force. For example, it can reduce the risk of arguments between parties, and small breakout groups can work in their own languages and then report back through a translator.

*Recording and monitoring*   If there are two facilitators, one might facilitate while the other records, or they swap roles periodically. Brainstormed lists and decisions might be presented back to the participants through flip charts, handouts, photographs, etc.

*Equipment*   The workshop may require flip charts, slide or overhead projectors, video equipment, tape-recorders, chalkboards and other equipment.

## Workshop methods

A wide variety of methods can be used in workshops. Switching between methods adds variety, alters the pace and allows mixing among the participants.
  Certain methods are better suited to particular activities. For example, brainstorming is more effective if done in small breakout groups; prioritizing options may be better done in plenary, where all the participants are together.

*Plenary sessions* gather everyone together. They are used at the beginning and end of a workshop, and at significant points in the middle. They work best when introducing ideas, reviewing progress, prioritizing options and demonstrating common ground across a whole group. If used too much, plenaries can be monotonous and may be dominated by a few individuals.

*Presentations* are a good way of building the participants' understanding of the overall process and the role of the facilitator. For example, different stakeholders might take turns to present the outputs of brainstorming sessions. This can help participants consider others' perspectives and adapt their own. Care is needed when deciding if there is enough goodwill for such presentations to be effective.

*Mini-lectures* may be useful in getting across condensed information in a short space of time. It is beneficial if soon afterwards the participants can begin to apply the approaches covered in the lecture to their own experiences. The mini-lecture may also provide a format for participants to present their perceptions of the conflict.

*Small groups* of four or more participants encourage intensive, creative study of one subject. They allow ideas to be expressed, discussed and developed quite freely. A limited time, with a specific focus on one or two issues, may work best. One person can be asked to act as a timekeeper and another as recorder who reports back during the plenary. To prevent stifling creativity, avoid having individuals who cannot work together in the same group.

*Pairs* encourage new, closer relationships. They are suited to sharing personal information and feelings. Facilitators often use pairs early in a workshop so that all participants feel they have related to someone else. This helps build their confidence.

*Triangles* are groups of three people, where the third person observes the other two. The roles are then switched, so that each of the three people in turn plays observer. This introduces the mode of neutral observer and gives participants experience in watching what causes tension between parties.

*Role-playing* involves asking participants to act out conflict situations. Usually these situations are different from the conflict actually being discussed. Role-playing must be handled sensitively, and time must be allowed so people can come out of their roles afterwards. In triangles, two people can act out their assigned roles while the third person observes and takes notes.

*Visualizing* is a workshop method of a different sort. Facilitators often find ways of visualizing the concepts, processes and options being discussed, for example as flow diagrams, maps or cluster diagrams. The process of selecting the type of diagram and developing it should be participative, with each participant reflecting on his or her own beliefs and values.

*Songs, dances and games* may be appropriate in certain circumstances and will be influenced by the participants' cultural mix.

# Chapter 14

# Managing difficult people

As stated in Chapter 6, 'difficult' people share the same demands as other stakeholders, but for various reasons have a voice of their own. There are many different types of difficult people. They may be overly critical, refusing to co-operate, fomenting discontent among other participants and obstructing the negotiation process. They may be aggressive, trying to force other participants to comply with their wishes. They may show off what they see as their superior knowledge and skills, dominating discussions and preventing others from contributing. Or they may act as a victim, calling out for attention and distracting the focus of discussion.

Knowing how to deal with such people is mainly a matter of experience and skill. However, stakeholders and facilitators can use certain techniques to understand the nature of the person's problem and move things forward (Ury, 1991).

The most important strategy is to try to determine what makes the person refuse to co-operate. Behind the difficult behaviour (cynic, bully, victim, show-off, etc.) often lie anger, hostility, fear and mistrust. The participant may dig in and attack the facilitator, not because he or she is unreasonable but because he or she knows no other way to negotiate. In his or her view, the only alternative is to give in – and he or she does not want to do that.

Frustrated and angered, the facilitator may feel like striking back. This will probably make the situation worse. Or the facilitator may feel like just giving in, hoping to be left alone. But this is not helpful either. Thus, the problem is not only the participant's behaviour, but also the facilitator's reaction.

## A strategy for managing difficult people

This strategy is adapted from Ury (1991).

*Don't react*   Control your own behaviour. Wait, regain your mental balance and clarify in your mind what it is you ultimately want to achieve.

*Disarm the participant*   Next you need to help the difficult person regain his or her own mental balance. You need to defuse his or her negative emotions (defensiveness, fear, annoyance, suspicion, hostility). These emotions may have already been defused by the participant's initial outburst and thus the matter is effectively over. If this is so, don't react and risk re-igniting the problem. But if the hostility is likely to continue, try to break through the person's resistance and get him or her to listen. For example, apologize for any misunderstanding, agree to consider the demands and arrange a time to do this.

*Change the game*   Once you have created a favourable negotiating climate, you need to get the participant to stop bargaining over demands and start exploring ways to meet both sides' underlying motivations. Thus, engage the participant in problem-solving, recognizing that your needs as a facilitator are now part of the process of consensual negotiation. For example, ask the rest of the group for time away from the workshop to develop these ideas. Or consider allocating the person to one of the support roles suggested in Figure 14.1.

*Make it easy to say yes*   Try to overcome the person's scepticism and guide him or her to a mutually satisfactory agreement. Begin by identifying solutions both sides can easily agree to. It may be important here for him or her to save face (i.e. to 'build golden bridges for the enemy to retreat over').

## TRAINING EXERCISE 14.1.
## MANAGING DIFFICULT PEOPLE

### Objective
To explore ways of managing difficult people in a workshop setting.

### Tasks
This exercise can only be attempted either after the simulation exercise (Training Exercise 11.1) has been completed or when it is sufficiently advanced.
1.   Divide the participants into small groups. Ask each group to identify which of the actors in the simulation exercise presents (or might present in the near future) difficulties for an effective negotiation.
2.   Each group identifies what type of people these are (refer to Figure 14.1).
3.   The group discusses how their behaviour might be channelled so they become more co-operative and constructive.
4.   The group discusses how they would, as facilitators, need to manage their own behaviour and reactions in order to achieve this co-operation.

*Make it hard to say no*  The participant may still believe that he or she can prevail through superior power. In these cases, you need to enhance your own negotiating power and use it to bring the person into collaborative negotiations – but do this without making an enemy who resists even more. For example, you may need to return to the ground rules (Chapter 15) and ask the whole group for these to be strengthened; restate your own objectives for the workshop; or discuss the implications for all concerned if a consensual agreement fails to materialize.

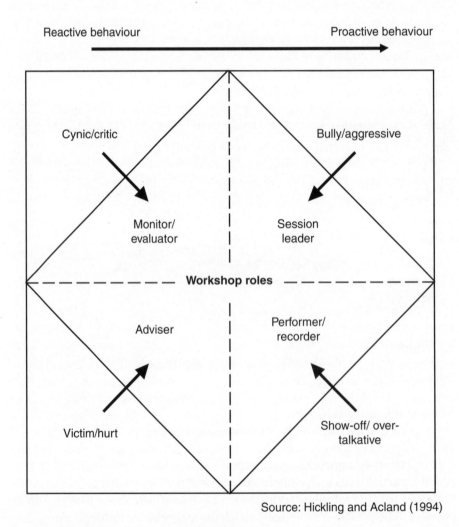

Source: Hickling and Acland (1994)

**Figure 14.1.**  Managing difficult people by providing workshop roles

# Chapter 15

# Consensual negotiation tools

This chapter describes some tools useful in consensual negotiations. They are divided into four groups: tools for building trust, for revealing underlying motivations, for widening and prioritizing options, and for reaching agreement. See Chapter 11 on when to use these tools during consensual negotiations.

Certain of these tools may also be useful at earlier stages in the conflict-management process, and other tools described elsewhere in this book may be useful during the negotiation phase.

It is unlikely that any set of negotiations will use all of the tools described here. The facilitator should select the most appropriate ones, and feel free to adapt them as required to suit the specific situation.

Much of the material in this chapter is adapted from the work of Hickling and Acland on behalf of the Environment Council (1994).

## Tools for building trust

### Warm-up

Warm-up sessions aim to introduce people to each other, lead them to develop some relationship and it is hoped, help them identify some immediate common interests, however tentative. Warm-ups provide a low-risk opportunity to meet others and feel safe among them. Common tools include the following.

*Round-table introductions*
Have each participant briefly introduce him- or herself to the group.

*Introductions by another participant*
Ask the participants to divide into pairs. One person in each pair interviews the other for five minutes, trying to find out as much about that person as possible. The two then swap roles, with the interviewee becoming the interviewer. After a second five minutes, ask the participants to introduce their

partners to the plenary group. This approach often works best if each person has to interview someone they have not met before.

*Workshop expectations*
Solicit the participants' expectations of the workshop. Ask each participant to speak in turn, then open the discussion to the floor.

In a highly hostile environment, or in formal situations, warm-ups must be designed with care. If they encourage the participants to be too intimate, people will resist them. In deciding whether to use a warm-up, think whether it will work. If in doubt, don't.

## Agenda building

If may be a good idea to have the group create the workshop agenda, or at least give them an input to amending and approving one that is already prepared. The idea is to give the participants a strong feeling of involvement from the outset, as well as to incorporate any unforeseen circumstances.

The participants should generate a list of what the group feels ought to be done, and then analyse it using two criteria: urgency (an opportunity will be missed if the item is not discussed soon), and significance (the overall impact of the item on managing the conflict). Avoid the risk of the agenda concentrating on the 'urgent' items but leaving out the 'significant' ones. Do not include items that are impossible to cover in the time available.

The agenda can start off with some items that stakeholders have agreed to previously, such as each party presenting the results of its analysis. Following these, the facilitator should try to integrate the other items suggested by the group into the overall three-phase strategy of the workshop: conflict analysis, widening options and reaching agreement (see Chapter 11). Note that it may not be necessary to describe these three phases to the participants – at least not at the start of the workshop.

## Ground rules

Ground rules are the rules the group needs to follow in order for the workshop to function well. They comprise the basic expectations of individual and group conduct during the workshop sessions. The facilitator may present a list of rules for the participants to approve – or better, invite the participants themselves to suggest rules. This encourages the participants to think about the importance of conduct, and collectively to create their own rules to follow during the workshop. Although the participants' attention will be on identifying the rules themselves, there is a hidden agenda here: to help the parties reach an early agreement. Early successes are important to build trust among the parties and to demonstrate that consensus is possible.

Some common ground rules are given below.

o   Allow each person to participate fully.
o   Listen to each person without interruption or disrespect.
o   Participants are free to suggest ideas and express feelings without ridicule.
o   All ideas accepted are valid options. Each one must be recorded to the satisfaction of the initiator.
o   Discussions may be confidential. For example, it may be agreed not to report to the whole group on sensitive issues that were discussed in pairs or small groups.
o   Discuss and agree the proposed agenda and timetable.
o   The group must recognize the overall 'worst alternative to a negotiated agreement' (e.g. escalation towards violence) and commit to working together to avoid it.
o   The group must accept the role of the facilitator.
o   Parties are free to ask for a time-out.
o   Meetings should start punctually.
o   All decisions, settlements and agreements must be reached through mutual consensus, not voting.
o   The participants must agree to a hierarchy of punishments if they break the rules, e.g. displeasure of the wider group, temporary suspension.

# Tools for revealing underlying motivations and interests

### Issue map

An issue map is a way of beginning to extract the underlying motivations and interests of the conflicting parties. Its advantage is that it displays results as they emerge. The technique is normally used in small groups (fewer than 15 people).

Each person receives four or five cards or sheets of sticky notepaper. Using a marker pen, he or she writes down ideas about the issue of concern – one idea per card. The cards from all participants are then posted on a board or the wall. Cards bearing similar ideas are clustered together, while those that are different are placed farthest apart.

Once the cards are clustered together, the facilitator asks the participants if any of their cards should be moved to a different position. In this way, the ideas can be grouped and regrouped until an optimum clustering is reached. It is important to stress that this is not voting, but a way of identifying areas where the participants share things in common.

Once the participants have understood the idea, the facilitator can stand back and let them develop the issue map by themselves.

An issue map is often used to identify common underlying motivations and interests in workshop expectations. It works best when combined with a particular style of questioning by the facilitator.

### Question strategies

The way a facilitator manages the exploration of issues is critical. Certain types of questions can encourage participants to pinpoint the true motivating factors. Table 15.1 identifies some styles of questioning designed to reveal underlying interests.

## Tools for widening and prioritizing options

The more potential solutions on the table, the easier it is to find one (or several) that will work. An adversarial approach to negotiation encourages parties to demand a single predetermined solution. Consensual negotiation, on the other hand, seeks to generate as many options as possible, so increasing the basis for an agreement. This section contains some ways of doing this.

### Brainstorming

Brainstorming is a way of getting a group to generate a lot of ideas quickly. It is a very flexible technique and can be used in a wide variety of situations (see Chapters 4 and 11). There are many different ways to do brainstorming. Here is a simple variant.

Participants begin by writing down ideas on a topic individually. Give them 5–10 minutes to do this.

The participants then move into small groups. Within each group, participants take turns to put forward one of the ideas they have written. Someone is appointed to write down the ideas on cards or a chalkboard, so everyone can see them. Ideas that are already written should not be repeated. The group continues to generate ideas until the flow of ideas ebbs or the time is up.

Finally the various groups' ideas are amalgamated and discussed in plenary. Seeing what other groups have proposed may stimulate participants to put forward yet more ideas.

**Table 15.1. Question strategies for revealing underlying motivations and interests**

| Approach | Purpose | Technique | Examples |
|---|---|---|---|
| **Encouraging** | | | |
| In the hope that participants begin to reveal interests | Convey interest, open up communication | Don't agree or disagree; use neutral words; ask questions with a positive tone | 'I see. What else happened?'<br>'Could you tell us a little more about this?' |
| **Paraphrasing** | | | |
| Restating in your words the speaker's message to reveal what you guess are the underlying interests | Show that you are listening and understanding; clarify meaning and interpretation | Restate the basic ideas, emphasizing facts | 'Let me see if I understand you'<br>'In other words…'<br>'So what you're saying is…' |
| **Acknowledging** | | | |
| Noting the deeper feelings that underlie the speaker's comments | Show that you are listening and understanding; help speaker evaluate his/her comments after hearing them expressed by someone else | Distinguish between substantive and emotional content of message; select a word or phrase that describes the exact feeling and level of intensity | 'So when X happened, you felt irritated'<br>'You seem to be very…' |
| **Reframing** | | | |
| Rewording the speaker's criticism or negative comment in the positive | Show that you are listening; defuse anger; identify the underlying needs and interests | Restate positively the speaker's intent, omitting charged words and accusations | Restate 'I'm getting really tired of these meetings; nothing ever happens…' as 'So you want meetings to have results. What might be an example of a positive result?' |
| **Summarizing** | | | |
| Condensing the main points of the speaker's overall message in the form of an interest | Review progress; pull together important ideas and facts | Restate and summarize the major ideas and feelings | 'Would I be right in thinking that these are the main ideas you have expressed so far…?' |

Source: Developed by A. Grzybowski of Alex Grzybowski and Associates, Sidney, BC, Canada (unpublished)

Brainstorming can be combined with other techniques, such as an issue map (see above), SWOT analysis and the prioritization methods discussed below.

Some rules for brainstorming:

o   No criticism of someone else's ideas: all ideas are valid.
o   Limit the time allowed for brainstorming, to encourage spontaneity and creativity. However, the limit should be flexible if new ideas are still flowing.
o   Keep ideas simple: no more than three words per idea. The detail can come later.
o   Write the options large enough for all participants to see, using marker pens on sticky notepaper or flip-chart paper. Write down the ideas as they are generated: seeing the others' ideas inspires creativity.
o   Combine ideas that are the same, and cluster those that are similar (for example, ideas that address the same problem or share the same level of uncertainty).

## Carousel

This technique (Hickling and Acland, 1994) is useful for brainstorming on a number of different topics at the same time. The meeting room is divided into a number of 'sites' where groups can sit and discuss. Each site is devoted to a particular topic and has a notice board or chalkboard.

The participants are divided into small groups, who are asked to brainstorm on the topics. Instead of staying in the same place, the groups rotate around the different sites. As the groups rotate, each reviews the results of the other groups' work and then adds their own ideas.

A facilitator or a member of each group stays at each site to explain the thinking behind the ideas and to cluster similar suggestions. The length of time allocated for each group at each site should be limited. However, more time will be needed for the first group at each site, since ideas sometimes take a while to start flowing.

## SWOT analysis

SWOT stands for **S**trengths, **W**eaknesses, **O**pportunities and **T**hreats. SWOT analysis is commonly used to study a policy, strategy or plan (or the lack of one), but can be used in a wide range of other situations. At the beginning of a project, SWOT analysis is likely to focus on the current situation and aim to develop a common view of a problem or conflict. A SWOT analysis may also be used to evaluate the likely effectiveness of a proposal; in such cases, it may focus on developing monitoring arrangements and cementing an emerging agreement.

The analysis aims to investigate the problem or proposal from both the inside and outside perspectives. The participants first identify the internal strengths and weaknesses relating to the topic, perhaps in the small groups using brainstorming techniques. They then identify the external opportunities and threats associated with the topic.

The major strengths and weaknesses are written in the top row of the matrix in Table 15.2. The main opportunities and threats are written in the left-hand column.

Following this, the participants identify ways to avoid or reduce the negative aspects (the weaknesses and threats) and to build on the positive ones (the strengths and opportunities). This is done in four steps:

○ **S–O analysis** How can the strengths be used to take advantage of the opportunities identified?
○ **S–T analysis** How can the strengths be used to counteract the threats?
○ **W–O analysis** How can the weaknesses be overcome to take advantage of the opportunities?
○ **W–T analysis** How can the weaknesses be overcome to counteract the threats?

Suggestions for each of these can be written in the relevant cells in Table 15.2.

## Ends–means analysis

Ends–means analysis is a way to identify options for reaching a desired end. The analysis starts with identification of a goal: a desirable end state of affairs (such as a secure cash income). In a conflict situation, this could be,

Table 15.2. Matrix for SWOT analysis

|  | **Strengths** Positive characteristics and advantages of the situation | **Weaknesses** Negative characteristics, disadvantages of the situation |
|---|---|---|
| **Opportunities** Outside factors that benefit the situation | **S–O analysis** How can the strengths be used to take advantage of the opportunities? | **W–O analysis** How can the weaknesses be overcome to take advantage of the opportunities? |
| **Threats** Outside factors that hinder the situation | **S–T analysis** How can the strengths be used to counteract the threats? | **W–T analysis** How can the weaknesses be overcome to counteract the threats? |

Source: IIRR (1996)

for example, some underlying need or value common to one or more of the parties.

The question is then posed: 'If this is the end goal, what are the means of achieving it?' The participants then brainstorm to identify a range of options (Figure 15.1).

When the brainstorming begins to slow down (i.e. all options are identified), ask: 'Now, if this original goal is thought of as a "means" and not an "end", what new goal are we trying achieve?' In the example in Figure 15.2, this is payment of school fees.

When the discussion slows down, the focus returns to identifying the means to achieve this new end (Figure 15.3).

## Prioritizing options

Various ways can be used to prioritize among the most promising options.

*PNI (positive, negative, interesting)* Once all the options are collected, each set of stakeholders or small, cross-stakeholder groups are asked to decide whether they see each option as positive, negative or just interesting. If the participants cannot agree, the option is put into the 'interesting' category. The aim is to identify options where there is common ground, either positive or negative. The positive ones can be taken forward and the negative ones rejected or modified.

*Traffic lights* This is similar to PNI, except that rather than small groups reaching consensus, each individual identifies the option that he or she sees as positive, negative or undecided. Coloured stickers are given to each participant: red for negative (i.e. stop), green for positive (go) and orange for undecided. Each person puts a sticker of the appropriate colour on each option. The technique is useful when it is too early in the process for small groups to be able to reach a consensus or if the hostility level is too high.

*Limited voting* The participants are each given three stickers (any colour will do). They put the stickers on their three most-favoured options. The facilitator must explain that this is not normal voting (i.e. it is not about majority rule), but simply a way of finding those options where some of the parties share a positive interest.

This technique works well without stickers: each participant is given three votes (or four or five) to allocate among the options as he or she wishes. The facilitator keeps a tally of the votes for each option.

*Direct ranking* The results of limited voting can be used to rank the options: for example, to decide which options to pursue first or which to drop.

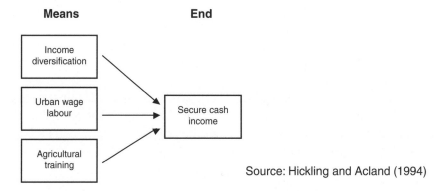

Source: Hickling and Acland (1994)

**Figure 15.1.** Example of initial stage of means–ends analysis.

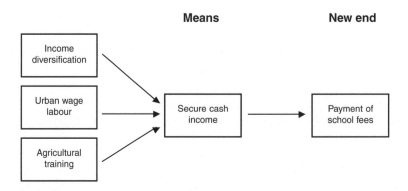

**Figure 15.2.** Example of middle stage of means–ends analysis

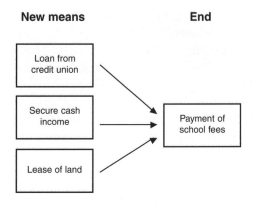

**Figure 15.3.** Example of final stage of means–ends analysis

*Pros and cons*   Each option is analysed in terms of its advantages (pros) and disadvantages (cons). These qualifications can be listed in two columns against each option. This is best done on an individual basis, with no direct criticism allowed of each person's suggestions.

*Pair-wise ranking*   Small groups compare each option against each of the others in turn. Through this process, they develop a set of evaluation criteria. They judge each option against the criteria and can then sit back and look for the options that stand out.

## Tools for reaching agreement

### Analysis of uncertainty

Uncertainty is always a key element in complex conflict situations. Analysing uncertainty in relation to options is an important step in building towards an agreement. If uncertainties are not discussed and understood, this can weaken agreements and bring the conflict-management process into disrepute.

Uncertainties can be divided into four types:

o   Uncertainties over **detail**: the timing, place, scale and type of action involved in the option.
o   Uncertainty over **effect**: the precise level and significance of the benefits the option is hoped to bring.
o   Uncertainties over **negative impact**: things that may be negatively affected by the option.
o   Uncertainties over **required support**: what needs to be put in place for the option to be effective.

Once the uncertainty has been classified into one or more of these categories, it can be analysed against two key criteria:

o   **Reducibility**   This is the amount of effort (time or money) needed to reduce the uncertainty, for example through studies, public participation, risk analysis or impact prediction.
o   **Relevance**   This is the extent to which an uncertainty makes it difficult for parties to support an option. Some uncertainties will be fundamental to this support (so must be reduced), while others will be negligible.

In narrowing further the promising options, the task is to look for uncertainties that are both relevant and easily reduced (Figure 15.4). Uncertainties that have low relevance can either be ignored or given low

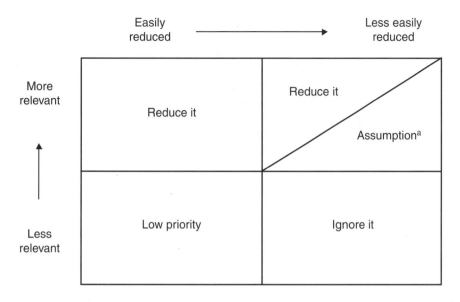

a *Assumption*: agree the principles and working assumptions that will enable the solution to be taken forward, despite the uncertainties.

Source: Hickling and Acland (1994).

**Figure 15.4.** Analysis of uncertainty

priority. This figure can be used to decide whether the uncertainty is manageable and therefore the option can be taken forward.

## Common grounding matrix

This technique is used to get acceptance on those options that have proven to be most promising. It involves: (a) amending options so that all parties accept them; and (b) bringing together different options into a single package. The common grounding matrix is probably the most important tool for a workshop approach to conflict management, since it is the focal point for developing a lasting agreement.

The matrix requires the parties to say whether they can accept each option or whether it must first be modified. For each option, the parties have three choices:

A   **Accepted**   The option is acceptable as currently stated.
R   **Rejected**   The option is unacceptable, and no amendment would make it acceptable.
Ac  **Accepted with conditions**   The option can be accepted but only if it is amended in a particular way.

**Table 15.3. Example of common grounding matrix**

| Decision area | Options | Stakeholder groups | | | | Taken forward |
|---|---|---|---|---|---|---|
| | | W | X | Y | Z | |
| 1 | a | A | A | R→Ac | A | Yes |
| | b | R | R | R | R | No |
| 2 | c | A | A | A | A | Yes |
| | d | R | A | A | A | No |
| | e | A | R→Ac | R→Ac | A | Yes |
| 3 | f | R | R | A | R | No |

Source: Hickling and Acland (1994)

The parties are first asked to assign only *A* (accept) or *R* (reject) to each option. The output of these choices is displayed in a matrix. Initial common ground is easily identified where all parties choose the same option or all reject an option (Table 15.3).

The focus then moves to building common ground where there is least difference, for example where only one party has rejected the option. The party is then asked: 'How would this option be amended to make it acceptable to you?'

Frequently the changes needed are quite minor, such as requests for changes in wording, or naming an agency or individual to verify the implementation of the option. But sometimes the changes are significant, in that they may affect the acceptability of the option to one of the other parties. Examples might include requesting that the option be piloted over a defined time period or in a specific location, or asking for compensation or a mitigation measure. In these cases, the amended option may need further changes.

The conditions associated with all changes are recorded and the option shifted from rejection *(R)* to conditional acceptance *(Ac)*.

If the options need to be restructured completely, the facilitator can break the participants into groups. The groups are charged with revising the difficult options in a form that all parties can accept. The groups' suggestions are then returned to the plenary workshop and the matrix session continues.

### Reality testing

Even if an option is acceptable to all, can it be implemented? Some of the criteria for this 'reality testing' are listed below.

Some of the quicker tests can be done during the workshop itself. The results are then presented to the participants, and any changes to the options and their conditions can be made accordingly.

Where tests need more time, they may need to be built into the overall agreement. For example, the agreement may be implemented as a pilot study, with the outcome presented to the participants at a later date.

*Criteria for reality testing*
o   Can the expectations that each party has of the agreement be fulfilled?
o   Are the options technically feasible?
o   Is there adequate finance or funding available?
o   Is the amount of time between the implementation of the agreement and the first benefits realistic?
o   Is this time short enough to encourage the stakeholders to continue their support for the agreement and any longer-term changes it requires?
o   Will the implementation pass any milestones that can be used to gauge progress?
o   Do the representatives' supporters approve of the agreement that has been reached?
o   Is the agreement politically viable?
o   Does the agreement include mechanisms to ensure that each party maintains its side of the agreement, e.g. independent monitoring or verification?

## Objectively verifiable indicators

A consensual agreement needs to include some way the parties can tell whether it is successful. A common approach is to determine 'objectively verifiable indicators' and to monitor these periodically after the agreement is put into effect.

These indicators are necessary to show whether a negotiated agreement is holding, or to measure the positive or negative impact of the agreement. If the agreement fails to live up to expectations, the indicators will show this and the parties can be invited back to discuss solutions.

An indicator might be anything from the number of fish in a stream (as a measure of water quality) to the amount of money entering a bank account (as a measure of income). Indicators should be objectively verifiable: anyone who observes them comes up with the same answer. This means they are unlikely to be subject to personal interpretation or bias.

Stakeholders often have diverse cultures: different values, language, wealth, status, decision making and so on. This makes it difficult to find indicators that everyone finds suitable. There are two ways of dealing with this:

o **Grand indicators**   These are very broad goals for which one or more indicators can be found. For example, the goal of reducing tension can be measured by the indicator 'no further sabotage to property'.

o **Individually acceptable indicators**   Parties with different cultures may agree to set their own indicators, but must choose those that are acceptable to the other parties.

## Commitment package

A commitment package is one way to present the agreement. Its strength lies in making the following specific:

o   the actions (i.e. the accepted options) that are agreed on

o   the types of further exploration needed before an action can be implemented

o   who is responsible for doing what

o   when it is to be achieved.

Figure 15.5 provides a form for a commitment package.

| | Commitment package | | | |
|---|---|---|---|---|
| | **Action** | **Exploration** | **Responsibility** | **Delivery date** |
| 1 | | | | |
| 2 | | | | |
| 3 | | | | |
| 4 | | | | |
| etc. | | | | |

Figure 15.5. Form for commitment package

# Appendix 1

## Briefing notes for Training Exercise 4.6 (Orange negotiations)

### *Orange negotiations*
### Briefing notes for Jack Smith

Your name is **Jack Smith**. You are a biologist/pharmacologist working for **Druginternat**, a multinational drugs company. Your latest success has been the discovery of a drug which when injected gives protection against rozenella. This is a new disease which is extremely dangerous for women in the later stages of pregnancy, and which invariably causes brain damage to the unborn child.

Unfortunately the disease is on the increase and an epidemic is forecast for this winter in the south of the country. The Minister of Health has requested that your firm mass-produce the drug in order to combat this outbreak. It is quite clear that without it, many hundreds of women will die and thousands of infants will be born with defects.

Curiously enough, the drug is produced from a combination of natural products, the main ingredient of which is found in the juice of oranges, but only that of the old variety 'Sunny', which is still grown in small quantities in rural Sicily.

Your firm has invested large sums in the development of this drug, which takes four months to produce. Now you and your firm are about to reap the rewards of your hard work and dedication. You are standing at the threshold of a golden future as the firm's leading scientist and you are looking forward to being a national celebrity.

After some considerable trouble you have found an importer, Mr Corleone, who has cornered the market and has a supply of 4000 'Sunny' oranges for sale at an exorbitant but affordable price of K12 000. You need only 3000 oranges to ensure a sufficient supply of the drug for the current campaign.

Unfortunately, when you contact Mr Corleone, he informs you that a Ms Simone West is also interested in purchasing the oranges for her firm, Envirochem Ltd, a competitor of your firm and with whom you have clashed in the past. There was even one matter over a disputed patent that led to a long and bitterly fought court case, which cost your firm a lot of money.

Your managing director has given you carte blanche to negotiate a deal with Ms West, and Mr Corleone has indicated that he is happy to go along with any agreement your two firms care to make, as long as he gets his money. You have K25 000 that you could use to buy the oranges you need.

One week ago Ms West sent you an invitation to meet at this office to sort things out, and today is the day!

## *Orange negotiations*
## Briefing notes for Simone West

Your name is **Simone West**. You are a biologist/environmental chemist working for **Envirochem**, a multinational chemical company.

Your latest success has been the discovery of a foam that can be sprayed on to chemical spillages. The foam not only neutralizes the toxins, but also facilitates the cleaning-up process afterwards. In recent trials, it demonstrated enormous potential against a whole range of toxic by-products, including dioxins and the diabolically dangerous polytetrahydroxyphenols.

It has recently emerged that a huge quantity of the latter substances have accumulated in the former Soviet Union as part of its chemical warfare programme. The Minister of Foreign Affairs has contacted your firm and requested that you mass-produce the new foam and place it at the disposal of the Russian government. The minister has secretly revealed that a storage facility is in immediate danger of releasing large quantities of the poison into the environment. This is threatening the lives of hundreds of thousands of the inhabitants of the city of Novosibirsk, as well as the important Taiga National Park, which was recently designated a world heritage site by the United Nations. The assessment is that you have less than one month to get the foam on site.

The foam is made from a combination of natural and synthetic products. The main natural ingredient is found in the skin of oranges, but only that of the old variety 'Sunny', which is still grown in small quantities in rural Sicily.

Your firm has invested large sums in the development and patenting of this foam, which takes only four days to produce. Now you and your firm are about to reap the rewards of your hard work and dedication. You are standing at the threshold of a golden future as the firm's leading scientist and you are looking forward to being acclaimed as a heroine by the Russian people.

After some considerable trouble you have found an importer, Mr Corleone, who has cornered the market and has a supply of 4000 'Sunny' oranges for sale at an exorbitant but affordable price of K12 000. You need only 3000 oranges to ensure a sufficient supply of the foam for the current crisis.

Unfortunately, when you contact Mr Corleone, he informs you that a Dr Jack Smith is also interested in purchasing the oranges for his firm, Druginternat Ltd. This is a competitor of your firm and you have clashed in the past. There was even one matter over a disputed patent that led to a long and bitterly fought court case, which cost your firm a lot of money.

Your managing director has given you carte blanche to negotiate a deal with Dr Smith, and Mr Corleone has indicated that he is happy to go along with any agreement your two firms care to make, as long as he gets his money. You have K25 000 that you could use to buy the oranges that you need.

One week ago you sent Dr Smith an invitation to meet at this office to sort things out, and today is the day!

# Appendix 2

## Briefing notes for Training Exercise 4.7 (Mining and wildlife reserve)

*Mining and the wildlife reserve*
**Briefing notes for Mr Brown of Enterprise Associates**

In a hidden valley, high in the tropical forests of the French protectorate of Papa Noveau, lies the newly gazetted 240 km$^2$ Flora Wildlife Reserve. Management of the reserve is the sole responsibility the Department of the Environment. Very recently a domestic mining company – Enterprise Associates – has begun to show interest in the possibility of mining valuable minerals within the reserve. As we speak, a representative of Enterprise Associates is on his way to visit the Department of the Environment to discuss the matter.

   **You are Mr Brown,** representative of Enterprise Associates and their principal public relations officer. You have a pleasant manner and people generally like you the first time they meet you. You have come to visit Dr Green of the Department of the Environment to seek permission for your company to explore for minerals within the Flora Wildlife Reserve. Your company's satellite imagery (remote sensing) data tell you that rich deposits of minerals are likely to be found in the lowland alluvial flood plains of the reserve. At this point in time you are asking permission only to explore the mining potential of the area. There is no decision as yet actually to mine the minerals.

   You are well aware that Dr Green will be reluctant to allow you permission to explore for minerals. However, you think that you might work around this by offering to grant his department a one-off payment. You have up to K100 000 to use for this purpose, but you know that your boss would like you to keep the amount as low as possible.

## *Mining and the wildlife reserve*
## Briefing notes for Dr Green of the Department of the Environment

In a hidden valley, high in the tropical forests of the French protectorate of Papa Noveau, lies the newly gazetted 240 km² Flora Wildlife Reserve. Management of the reserve is the sole responsibility the Department of the Environment. Very recently a domestic mining company – Enterprise Associates – has begun to show interest in the possibility of mining valuable minerals within the reserve. As we speak, a representative of Enterprise Associates is on his way to visit the Department of the Environment to discuss the matter.

**You are Dr Green**, Director of the Department of the Environment. Ultimately, all decisions regarding conservation within the country rest with you. You are particularly happy that the reserve has been gazetted, since the upper reaches of the watershed within the reserve are home to the habitat of the very rare one-footed blue parrot. There are, however, no other species of particular rarity or importance within the reserve.

You have been told that Mr Brown has come to visit you about mining for minerals in the reserve. You are extremely unhappy about this. You therefore have very little interest in talking to him, except that you are aware that he may be about to offer your department some sort of financial incentive. This incentive is most definitely of interest to you since your department's budget is soon to be drastically cut. Without a rapid injection of around K100 000, it will be impossible for your department to manage those upland habitats within the reserve, which are so critical to the long-term protection of the one-footed blue parrot.

# Appendix 3

## Briefing notes for Training Exercise 11.1 (Coralbay Coastal Resource Management Project)

### General briefing notes

#### The project

On the small island of Atol in the Indian Ocean, a local NGO – the Social Concern Agency (SCA) – has been funded by the Swedish aid agency to provide environmental management skills and opportunities to communities in the coastal district of Coralbay. The issues to be addressed by the two-year programme relate to coastal resource management, and are likely to include forestry management, fish-stock rehabilitation, livestock husbandry, coral aquaculture and mangrove protection.

Coralbay district has its main centre at Cook Town, which in turn has good transport links to the island's main commercial centre at Atol City. Income for the people living in the rural area comes from logging, fishing and dairy cattle. Because of its close proximity to Atol City, the natural resources of the district have been exploited by government agencies and private companies. The landowners and local resource users have benefited little. The resources in question include forests, various non-timber forest products, fish, coral, shells and grazing lands.

The project aims to put the management of these resources into the hands of the traditional landowners and resource users. Through this, it is hoped to build employment opportunities, promote sustainable natural resource management and add value to the use of resources before they are exported from the district.

# The conflict

The district of Coralbay comprises five dispersed settlements and Cook Town (population 2500). The settlements are scattered along the coast around Coralbay. The bay is a shallow, coral-rich body of water fringed by mangroves.

Three years ago, under guidance from the Fisheries Department, the area chief placed a total fishing ban on the bay. The ban lasted one year. Since then, fish species that had been absent for many years began to be observed. The total ban has now been lifted for all but the breeding season (October to February). However, nets of only a specific mesh size are allowed in the bay, to give the re-emerging fish stocks a chance to reach adulthood.

Fish wardens – people appointed from these settlements – are authorized to police the waters for illegal fishing and undersized nets. Conflict has arisen between those community groups who want to fish during the breeding season and use finer nets, and those who wish to respect the restrictions.

Other conflicts have arisen as certain individuals have been found to be using undersized nets. Two fishermen have been attacked by a mob for fishing at night during the breeding season, and a number of boats have been damaged.

The situation is in danger of escalation, not least because of outstanding land disputes that had lain dormant until the recent troubles began.

# Stakeholder groups

An initial analysis of the conflict by SCA identified six key parties with whom it might be possible to negotiate to prevent the violence from escalating and to end it:

o   Coralbay Fishing Association
o   Coralbay District Council
o   Area chief and subchiefs
o   Fisheries Department
o   Fish wardens
o   SCA.

Other parties who were considered potentially important to the management of the conflict (e.g. in providing opportunities or blocking any proposals), included landowners, council of elders, the women's association and the Forestry Department. These parties will not be part of the initial collaborative negotiation, but may be called upon as and when needed.

## Existing mechanisms

Representatives of those members of the Fishing Association who are in favour of the continuing restrictions have been to the chief to ask him to solve the difficulties and stop the violence. His response was that the cash incentives for fishing during the breeding season were insurmountable, as no other source of cash income is available at this time.

When it approached the District Council, the Association was advised to try to bring those breaking the ban in front of the local magistrate. However, this was seen as too divisive and would probably cause further bad feeling.

Under normal circumstances, such conflicts would be resolved through the chief convening a meeting of the council of elders drawn from the five settlements; this group would reach a consensus on how to break the deadlock. The conflicting parties generally view this council as impartial. It reaches consensus in three steps: an initial meeting where the elders speak to each group separately and encourage the parties to be reasonable in their demands; a second meeting where each side puts its case and ideas for resolution; and a final meeting where elders make their deliberation. Agreements reached over the last few years have usually been documented.

## Conflict-management plan

SCA has already analysed the conflict in a participatory way with each of the stakeholder groups, enabling each party to identify their underlying motivations (needs, fears, etc.). Each party has agreed to send representatives along to a two-day workshop. The workshop is to be facilitated by two staff from SCA, both viewed by the communities as outside and impartial. At this point, it is not considered necessary to train community leaders in facilitation and mediation skills. If the workshop proves successful, then it will be used as a springboard for demonstrating the benefits of community training in conflict management. This training could be implemented at a later date. In an effort to create a level playing field for negotiation, the two-day workshop will begin with each party presenting its understanding of the conflict. However, additional issues are likely to come to light only later in the workshop.

## Coralbay Coastal Resource Management Project
## Brief for representatives of the
## Coralbay Fishing Association

### Background

Coralbay is a coastal area of about five square miles. Over the past 20 years, fishermen have experienced reduced catch volumes, a loss of species diversity, a reduction in the average size of fish caught and a reported slowing of the growth rate of individual fish. The Coralbay Fishing Association was registered five years ago to co-ordinate fishing in and around Coralbay and to try to turn around this decline. The onset of the total fishing ban three years ago loosened the friendship and co-operation among the members. Although the total ban was lifted two years ago, a ban on fishing in the main breeding season (from October to February) remains. In addition, net mesh sizes have been limited to a minimum of 100 mm.

No member in the Association admits to breaking the breeding-season ban or net-size restrictions, but at least one-third of the members are involved in one or other of these activities. Frustrated by those breaking the ban, a minority of members have been responsible for acts of aggression towards those who are flouting the restrictions and have damaged a number of fishing boats.

### Roles

*Note: Mr Rich and Mr Poor are not allowed to see each other's briefs.*

#### Chairman of the Association (Mr Rich)
Well-educated, generally supports the fishing restrictions and wishes to see stocks returned to their historically high levels. As well as his two sons continuing to fish for the family (outside the breeding season), he has a secure year-round income from dairy farming. He is not really concerned one way or the other about resolving the conflict, except that he rather enjoys his privileged position in the community and would not like to see this undermined by violence. He knows nothing of SCA's Coralbay resource management project.

#### Association secretary (Mr Poor)
Spokesman for those disillusioned members of the Association who wish to see the continuing restrictions lifted. Mr Poor will not admit that he himself has ever broken the ban or net-size restrictions or is involved in violence or damage to boats, but he does 'fully understand and empathize with' the motives of those who do. Like many of those breaking the restrictions, he has a family to feed, clothe and send to school, and has no other secure income during the period of the ban from October to February. He knows nothing of SCA's Coralbay resource management project.

## Coralbay Coastal Resource Management Project
## Brief for representatives of the
## Coralbay District Council

### Background

The District Council comprises elected members from each of the five settlements along the coast, as well as three representatives from Cook Town. The council is the main local institution involved with SCA in planning the Coralbay Coastal Resource Management Project.

The council members are aware that their positions are due for re-election next month. Each is therefore keen to demonstrate active support for those likely to vote for them. About half of the area's eligible voters are in favour of the continuing restrictions and half are against.

### Roles

*Note: Mrs Left and Mr Right are not allowed to see each other's briefs.*

#### Chairperson of the Council (Mrs Left)

She has a strong constituency among the poor in the coastal settlements. As such, she is a vocal advocate of the need to reduce the allowable net sizes so that smaller fish can be caught, thereby boosting fish sales and local incomes. However, she recognizes that the restrictions currently have the support of the Department of Fisheries and are therefore unlikely to be changed. She calculates that if she can secure alternative income-earning opportunities for the poor in her constituency for the period October to February (i.e. when the ban is in place), then she may be able to hold on to her position on the council. Hence she is currently working closely with SCA to see if it can help.

#### Other leading voice on the council (Mr Right)

He is hoping to be re-elected by being seen to support the fishing restrictions currently in place. His real motivation for this is that if he can show that his support for the restrictions helped regenerate fish stocks, then when the election comes around again in two years' time, he will emerge as 'the one who saved the bay' and will be elected as council chairperson. In the meantime, he will not support any arrangement that may mean he is voted out in the elections next month.

# Coralbay Coastal Resource Management Project
## Brief for representative of the
## area chief and subchiefs

## Background

The area chief and the subchiefs have seen their traditional authority eroded over the past few years as those with cash (such as Mr Rich) become more important and influential. However, the chief still commands a great deal of respect, especially from the poorer families in the district.

## Role

### Area chief (Chief Honcho)
He has agreed to represent the subchiefs at the two-day workshop. Though he would never say so in public, he does not object to his people fishing during the breeding period and has been known to accept small gifts for his silent support of these actions.

The reason he is attending the workshop is because he believes that it might offer a way for him and the subchiefs to enhance their declining importance. In particular, he expects to secure a good deal for the poorer families of the district and thereby make them feel indebted to him, so raising his status. The chief is not corrupt by nature. He is driven by a desire to bring back some of the traditional values and respect that he and his forefathers once enjoyed. Enhancing his wealth by receiving gifts or favours is the only way that he can see of achieving this. If questioned on the subject of gifts, he will, however, strongly deny receiving any.

## Coralbay Coastal Resource Management Project
## Brief for representative of the Fisheries Department

### Background

The Fisheries Department is responsible for the fish-stock surveys and quantitative analysis that led to the decision to lift the total fish ban in Coralbay two years ago, but to retain limits on net size and a ban during the breeding season. The period October to February was chosen for the ban because this is the breeding period of the bubblefish, the species most in need of rejuvenation in the bay. However, there are other fish (particularly tuna, which can be caught with 500 mm nets) present in sufficient numbers to be harvested all year round if the overall offtake is kept low.

### Role

#### Field officer (Mrs Calculus)
She visits Coralbay every week to find out from the chief and the fish wardens how the restrictions are working, and to collect survey data. She is concerned to see the restrictions working properly, but is ultimately interested only in the numbers of bubblefish, since this is the species most in need of rejuvenation. If she fails to bring about a measurable increase in the population of bubblefish by the year's end, she is unlikely to receive promotion within the department.

## Coralbay Coastal Resource Management Project
## Brief for representatives of the fish wardens


### Background

There are six fish wardens employed by the Department of Fisheries, each paid a small wage to ensure that no one fishes during the period October to February. Three of these six are retained year-round to ensure that net sizes meet the restrictions laid down when the total fish ban was lifted. The wardens all come from the poorer households in the district and are all fishermen themselves. Rumour has it that the reason some of the members of the Coralbay Fishing Association are breaking the restrictions is because some of the wardens are doing the same.


### Role

*Spokesperson for the fish wardens (Mr Baton)*
He is content that he and his wardens are doing everything in their power to enforce the restrictions. He is, however, upset that they are paid so little and that his work takes him away from his family for such long periods of time. He will fiercely defend himself and his wardens against any charges of colluding with other fishermen to break the restrictions, although he is secretly suspicious that two of his men may be doing just that.

He and the other wardens took the job for the status that it gives them in their settlements, as well as the cash that it brings during October to February, when other income is not available. If some way could be found to increase the wardens' pay, he feels sure that any collusion between the wardens and the fishermen would cease.

## *Coralbay Coastal Resource Management Project*
## Brief for representatives the
## Social Concern Agency (SCA)

### Background

SCA is a long-standing and well-respected NGO. It is staffed by local people and funded by both domestic and international donors. SCA has a good
track record in implementing community-based natural resource management projects, particularly in the forestry, fishing and livestock sectors. The
NGO also manages a number of community healthcare projects, including
a fully funded programme to build small clinics. The latter programme has
yet to reach the Coralbay area.

The Coastal Resource Management Project is intended to turn the Coralbay
natural environment around, from one where resources are continuously
degrading to one where they are used sustainably. At the same time, the
intention is to economically uplift the poorest households around the bay. It
aims to do this by, for example, encouraging the processing of timber, non-
timber forest products, fish and milk before these products are sent to Cook
Town and beyond. The project is designed to be process-led. That is to say,
although the overall objectives are defined, how to achieve them will be
determined as the project progresses. There is therefore a considerable degree of flexibility in how the funds can be spent.

### Role

#### *Project manager (Miss Care)*

She is a dedicated individual, highly educated and energetic. This is her
first appointment as a project manager, and she fears that the project might
not be successful. She dearly wishes to see the current fishing conflict resolved, not least because it is preventing her from building rapport with the
fishermen – rapport she needs to be able to begin the project.

Her style of management is one of actively encouraging individuals and
groups to come up with their own ideas. She will consider all ideas for re-
habilitating and managing the various natural resources that fall under the
project objectives. Funds can be released quickly, but only if they are used
for investment, e.g. for equipment or loans. Her budget cannot be used for
wages.

She has developed a good working relationship with the manager of SCA's
health clinic programme, and has had some success in placing Coralbay as
next on the list for a community health clinic.

# Appendix 4

# Briefing notes for Training Exercise 11.1 (Tukubu Conservation Area)

## General briefing notes

### The conflict

In a remote corner of Pigeon Island in the South Pacific, Agricultural Enterprise Ltd (AEL) wishes to establish a 5000 ha rubber plantation by clear-felling an area of tropical lowland forest. The site selected falls within the boundaries of the Tukubu Conservation Area, a 250 km² river basin proposed as a protected area by the government's Department of the Environment. The plantation site covers approximately half of the lowland flood plain of the Tukubu river basin.

Although the full biodiversity value of the Tukubu Conservation Area is not yet known, it is expected that the majority of the area's critical habitats will fall within this same lowland zone. In particular, bird surveys conducted by Dr Strangelove in the 1950s suggest that as many as 20 of the world's 43 species of endangered birds of paradise are to be found within this one lowland forest.

As a direct result of the AEL proposals, the land where the rubber plantation may be established is now the subject of a dispute between two indigenous clans: the Tukubu-West people and Tukubu-East people. Many months of consultation and negotiation have been held among all the parties.

The Department of the Environment and the Ministry of Agriculture have jointly invited a local NGO, the Agency for People and the Environment (APE), for assistance. APE, which is skilled in conflict management, is to help create a resource management plan for the Tukubu Conservation Area. A two-day workshop is to be held to develop the plan.

## Stakeholder groups

APE's initial analysis of the conflict identified six key stakeholder groups. These groups need to be involved in preparing the resource management plan if it is to have any chance of being effective and sustainable.

APE has already undertaken five months of office-based conflict analysis, participatory conflict analysis and community training with the Tukubu communities, consultation with all other stakeholder representatives and awareness-raising through the local media.

Everything is now in place for the workshop. Each of the six stakeholder groups has named two representatives to represent their interests at the workshop. Drawing on recent training in negotiation skills, the two land-owning groups have formed common (but different) positions on their land claims. The stakeholder groups and representatives are as follows:

*Agricultural Enterprise Limited*
o   Mr Bruce Outback (Director)
o   Dr Kafa Mubi (Technical specialist)

*Tukubu-West Landowners Association*
o   Mrs Elizabeth Araho (Chairperson)
o   Mr Pahai Maboroga (Secretary)

*Tukubu-East Landowners Association*
o   Mr Sirigi Mano (Chairperson)
o   Ms Ira Wagara (Secretary)

*Ministry of Agriculture*
o   Mr Walter Palmer (First secretary to a junior minister)
o   Mr Stanley Busse (Technical adviser)

*Department of the Environment*
o   Mr Tori Kanion (Deputy director)
o   Dr Simon Fawn (Conservation specialist)

*Delegation of the European Union*
o   Mrs Simone Blanch (Assistant to head of delegation)
o   Dr Luigi Dolomite (Natural resources adviser)

## Tukubu Conservation Area
## Brief for representatives of
## Agricultural Enterprise Ltd (AEL)

### Mr Bruce Outback (Director)
### Dr Kafa Mubi (Technical specialist)

Your company has recently completed a survey to identify the suitability of land in Pigeon Island to establish plantations of rubber trees. A 5000 ha site within the Tukubu Conservation Area was identified by the survey as 'the highest-quality land available'. Nearby were three alternative sites of slightly lower quality. All three alternatives lie outside the conservation area, and each is predicted to return a 15 per cent net annual profit over 20 years. In contrast, the conservation area site is expected to return a more healthy 30 per cent profit per year. Although you would like to plant all 5000 ha, you could still make 30 per cent profit on anything over 2500 ha. Below 2500 ha and the profit margin would slip to 25 per cent.

AEL's survey considered only biophysical data and did not take account of social or environmental factors. It is for this reason that your company has decided to attend the workshop. You are interested in seeing whether there are social and environmental problems in the Tukubu Conservation Area that indicate that you should move your investment to one of the three alternative sites. However, you maintain the hope that the proposed resource management plan for the Tukubu Conservation Area will enable you to establish the plantation in this area. You therefore intend to keep your knowledge of the alternative sites quiet unless the need arises.

Managing rubber plantations requires labour in the form of rubber tappers. This is a semi-skilled job, and you hope to be able to train local people and employ them to do this work on the plantation. You see the offer of employment to the local population as your most effective incentive for their co-operation and acceptance of the plantation.

You are not expecting these rural people to argue for a percentage share in the profits of the enterprise. However, if this matter is raised, you intend to do your best to push the discussion away from profit sharing and towards the offer of employment.

# Tukubu Conservation Area
## Brief for representatives of
## Tukubu-West Landowners Association

### Mrs Elizabeth Araho (Chairperson)
### Mr Pahai Maboroga (Secretary)

The Tukubu-West Landowners Association has recently taken legal advice from an independent land mediator from outside the province on its land-ownership claim in the Tukubu Conservation Area. The advice suggests that the Tukubu-West people have a stronger claim to the area proposed by AEL for the rubber plantation than do the people of Tukubu-East.

The Association has also decided that, in line with events in other areas of the country, they want to strike a deal with AEL to lease their land for a 5 per cent share of the profits. The members intend to hold out for both the full land claim and 5 per cent share. However, if the pressure becomes too great, they are willing to give a little on both counts. This is because some of the Association members are related by marriage to the Tukubu-East people and do not want to cause unnecessary conflict by keeping the Tukubu-East Landowners Association out of the profit-sharing altogether.

The Association will, however, fight to the end to stop the Tukubu-East people from claiming that they own the land belonging to the Tukubu-West people.

The Association's interest in AEL is not only about cash. The Tukubu-West people desperately want to earn a sustainable income to support their families. As a community, they also need education and better health services. A share of the profits from the AEL rubber plantation offers the best opportunity they have yet seen for these services to become a reality.

Field staff from the Department of the Environment have recently been in the region raising awareness of the advantages and disadvantages of AEL's proposal. As a result, the Association has noted concern among its members that although the land will only be leased to AEL, the intended clear-felling means that their hunting lands will be lost forever.

In addition, the Department tells them that they will no longer be able to collect fruits, wild crops, medicinal plants and other non-timber products. It has further come to their attention that the pesticides to be used on the plantation may lead to problems with fishing stocks in the rivers adjacent to the plantation.

## *Tukubu Conservation Area*
## Brief for representatives of
## Tukubu-East Landowners Association


### Mr Sirigi Mano (Chairperson)
### Ms Ira Wagara (Secretary)

The Tukubu-East Landowners Association has heard about the proposed AEL rubber plantation and is keen to receive a share of the profits by leasing AEL its land. Although the Tukubu-East people have historical evidence supporting their claim to the land where the plantation is proposed, they are aware that the claim of the Tukubu-West people is far stronger. Despite this, they are still expecting to gain some share of the rubber profits. Their hope is for a cut of around 5 per cent of the profits per year.

The Association's interest in AEL is not only about cash. The Tukubu-East people desperately want to earn a sustainable income to support their families. As a community, they also need education and better health services. A share of the profits from the AEL rubber plantation offers the best opportunity they have yet seen for these services to become a reality.

Field staff from the Department of the Environment have recently been in the region raising awareness of the advantages and disadvantages of AEL's proposal. As a result, the Association has noted concern among its members that although the land will only be leased to AEL, the intended clear-felling means that their hunting lands will be lost forever.

In addition, the Department tells them that they will no longer be able to collect fruits, wild crops, medicinal plants and other non-timber products. It has further come to their attention that the pesticides to be used on the plantation may lead to problems with fishing stocks in the rivers adjacent to the plantation.

## Tukubu Conservation Area
## Brief for representatives of the
## Ministry of Agriculture


### Mr Walter Palmer (First secretary to a junior minister)
### Mr Stanley Busse (Technical adviser)

The Ministry is keen to see the development of rubber as an export crop. The world price for rubber has remained consistently high and is predicted to do so for the foreseeable future. In particular, the climate of Pigeon Island makes it ideal for rubber, the highest yields for which come from plantations in lowland flood plains.

Two years ago the Ministry held secret talks with Expat Industries Incorporated (EII). This joint public/private venture (which operates under the name of Agrex Holdings Limited) has secured borrowings of K25 million, half in the form of a loan, half raised through a share flotation. This capital is to be used to construct a rubber processing and refining plant at Port Idyllic on the island's remote south coast. To repay the loan and return dividends to the shareholders, Agrex will need a substantial supply of raw rubber.

Construction of the plant is ahead of schedule. The Ministry, as the main investor, is keen to meet its target of 75 000 ha of viable rubber plantations across Pigeon Island within the next two years. This is the land area needed for the plant to return a profit. The AEL proposal in the Tukubu Conservation Area is important to the Ministry, since of late, the target of 75 000 ha has seemed unlikely to be met in time.

## Tukubu Conservation Area
## Brief for representatives of the
## Department of the Environment

### Mr Tori Kanion (Deputy director)
### Dr Simon Fawn (Conservation specialist)

The Department of the Environment has proposed the Tukubu Conservation Area as a 'wildlife preserve', thereby affording it legal protection under government legislation. The legislation states that clear-felling in wildlife preserves is strictly prohibited. The only protected areas legislation that allows for clear-felling is where the area is designated as a 'nature reserve'. In these cases, a resource management plan must be drawn up, detailing the zones to be targeted for clear-felling and outlining how the funds so generated would be used to promote nature conservation within the reserve.

When asked to defend the Department's desire for the Tukubu Conservation Area to be designated as a wildlife preserve, the staff proudly point to the country's national environmental management action plan (NEMAP), prepared by the Department after Pigeon Island signed the Biodiversity Convention in Rio in 1992. The key passage of text usually cited is as follows:

> 'Lowland rain forest constitutes our country's greatest wealth and yet is under the greatest threats. It is probably the most valuable long-term natural asset the country possesses. Research has shown that hunting for food for the protein it provides, and harvesting wild plants, brings immeasurably more value to the local community than selling off the logging rights or converting the forest to cash crops.' (Pigeon Island NEMAP, 1993, p. 87)

As well as being home to a number of rare species of birds of paradise, the lowland tropical forest present in the Tukubu Conservation Area is likely to host many plants of medicinal value. The Department is currently engaged in a programme to survey the commercial value of medicinal plants in the Tukubu Conservation Area. It has begun the survey by focusing on the same area proposed by AEL for the rubber plantation.

## Tukubu Conservation Area
## Brief for representatives of the
## Delegation of the European Union


### Mrs Simone Blanch (Assistant to head of delegation)
### Dr Luigi Dolomite (Natural resource adviser)

The EU Delegation has a K60 million, five-year development co-operation agreement with the Government of Pigeon Island. These funds are to be spent on an agreed programme of projects, primarily in the construction, agriculture and mining sectors. Most recently, the EU has provided financial assistance from the fund to develop the export potential of Pigeon Island for processed agriculture products. For example, the EU has loaned the Ministry of Agriculture K5 million for the construction of a rubber processing and refining plant at Port Idyllic. It is expecting a return on its investment.

There is little flexibility for the EU to be able to shift funds in the development co-operation agreement from the pre-established programmes. However, the Delegation has a Small-Scale Project Initiative budget line available to support local community development projects up to a maximum of K50 000 per project per year.

The Delegation is staffed by a team of rather inexperienced professionals. Most of these are trained as economists. The only exception is the natural resource adviser, who, at 30, has just completed a PhD on birds of paradise in the rainforests of Bolivia.

The role of Mrs Simone Blanch (assistant to the head of the delegation) is to ensure that the development co-operation agreement is implemented as intended and on time, and to demonstrate that monies have been successfully allocated from the Small-Scale Project Initiative. If she achieves these goals, her chances of returning to Brussels to a more senior position (and a second house in the Loire Valley) are greatly increased.

# References

Below are references cited in the text, as well as some other useful further reading.

Buckles, D. (ed.) (1999) *Cultivating Peace: Conflict and Collaboration in Natural Resource Management*, International Development Research Centre, Ottawa, and World Bank Institute, Washington, DC.

Bush, K. (1998) *A Measure of Peace: Peace and Conflict Impact Assessment of Development Projects in Conflict Zones*, Working Paper 1, Peacebuilding and Reconstruction Program Initiative, IDRC, Ottawa.

Carney, D. (1999) Approaches to Sustainable Livelihood for the Rural Poor, *ODI Poverty Briefing* 2, Overseas Development Institute, London.

Chambers, R. (1997) Participatory Rural Appraisal (PRA): Analysis of Experience, *World Development*, vol. 22 (9), pp. 1253–68.

Chupp, M. (1991) 'When Mediation Is Not Enough', *MCS Conciliation Quarterly*, pp. 2–3, 12–13.

Craig, G., Hall, N. and Mayo, M. (1998) Editorial Introduction: Managing Conflict through Community Development, *Community Development Journal*, vol. 33(2), pp. 77–79.

De Bono, E. (1999) *Six Thinking Hats*. Little Brown, Boston, Mass.

DFID (1997) Conflict Reduction through British Co-operation: A Briefing for Agencies Seeking Support for Conflict Reduction Activities, Department for International Development, London.

Doucet, I. (1996) *Resource Pack for Conflict Transformation*, International Alert, London. Available from International Alert, 1 Glyn Street, London, tel: +44 207 793 8383, fax: +44 207 793 7975, e-mail: general@international-alert.org

Fisher, R., Kopelman, E. and Kupfer Schneider, A. (1994) *Beyond Machiavelli: Coping with Conflict*, Harvard University Press, Cambridge, MA.

Fisher, R. and Ury, W. (1987) *Getting to Yes: Negotiating Agreement Without Giving In*, Arrow Books, London.

Goodhand, J. and Hulme, D. (1997) *NGOs and Complex Political Emergencies*, Working Paper 1, University of Manchester and INTRAC, Oxford.

Harriss, J. and de Renzio, P. (1997) 'Missing Link or Analytically Missing? The Concept of Social Capital', in Harriss, J. (ed.) (1997) *Policy Arena: Social Capital*, unpublished, Development Studies Institute, London School of Economics, London.

Hickling, A. and Acland, A. (1994) *Professional Training for Facilitators and Mediators: Course Handbook*, Environment Council, London.

Hobley, M. and Shah, K. (1996) What Makes a Local Organisation Robust? Evidence from India and Nepal, *Natural Resource Perspectives* vol. 11, Overseas Development Institute, London.

ICIMOD (1996) Seminar on Conflict Resolution in Natural Resources, International Centre for Integrated Mountain Development, Kathmandu.

IIRR (1996) *Recording and Using Indigenous Knowledge: A Manual*, International Institute of Rural Reconstruction, Silang, The Philippines.

IUCN (1995) Reaching Agreement: Conflict Resolution Training for the IUCN, International Union for Conservation and Nature, Geneva.

Lederach, J.P. (1994) *Building Peace, Sustainable Reconciliation in Divided Societies*, UN University, Tokyo.

Lederach, J.P. (1996) The Mediator's Cultural Assumptions, *MCS Conciliation Quarterly*.

McDonald, J. (1994) The Application of Alternative Dispute Resolution Techniques to Environmental Planning Disputes, *Environmental Liability*, pp. 134–46.

McIlwaine, C. (1998) Contesting Civil Society: Reflections from El Salvador, *Third World Quarterly*, vol. 9(4).

McIntosh, D., Jones, S. and Warner. M. (2000) South Pacific Conflict Management Project, Final Report to the Department for International Development, Conflict and Humanitarian Assistance Department, Department for International Development, London.

Moore, C. (1996) *The Mediation Process: Practical Strategies for Resolving Conflict*, 2nd edn, Jossey-Bass, San Francisco, Calif.

Moore, C. and Santosa, A. (1995) Developing Appropriate Environmental Conflict Management Procedures in Indonesia: Integrating Traditional and New Approaches, *Cultural Survival International* Fall, pp.23–9.

Ndelu, T. (1998) Conflict Management and Peace Building through Community Development, *Community Development Journal* vol. 33(2), pp. 109–16.

ODI (1998) 1st Interim Report to the Department for International Development, South Pacific Conflict Management Project, Overseas Development Institute, London.

OECD (1998) *Conflict, Peace and Development Co-operation on the Threshold of the 21st Century*, Development Cooperation Guidelines Series, Organisation for Economic Development and Cooperation, Paris.

O'Reilly (1998) *The Contribution of Community Development to Peace-Building: World Vision's Area Development Programmes*, World Vision, London.

PEACE Foundation Melanesia (1998) Manual for Community Development Training Program, unpublished, Port Moresby, Papua New Guinea.

Pretty, J., Guijt, I., Scoones, I. and Thompson, J. (1995) *A Trainer's Guide for Participatory Learning and Action*, International Institute of Environment and Development, Sustainable Agriculture Programme, London.

Putman, R. (1993) *Making Democracy Work: Civic Traditions in Modern Italy*, Princeton University Press, Princeton, NJ.

Resolve, Inc. (1994) *The Role of Consensus-Building in Community Forestry*, Resolve/FAO, Washington, DC.

Scott, A., Lewis, M., Chaffey, D., Warner, M. and Webster, D. (1998) Bolivia: Pilon Lajas Agroforestry Project: Output to Purpose Review, 21 September–6 October 1998, Department for International Development, UK.

Ury, W. (1991) *Getting Past No: Negotiating with Difficult People*, Century Business, London.

Warner, M. (1995) Approach to Community Planning: The Case of a Rural Community in Belize, *PLA Notes* 23, International Institute for Environment and Development, Sustainable Agriculture Programme, London.

Warner, M. (1999) Conflict Impact Assessment, discussion paper for the Conflict and Humanitarian Assistance Department, UK Department for International Development, London.

Warner, M. and Jones, P. (1998) Assessing the Need for Managing Conflicts in Community-Based Natural Resource Projects, *ODI Natural Resources Perspective Paper* 35, Overseas Development Institute, London.

Warner, M., Robb, C., Mackey, A. and Brocklesby, M. (1996) Linking PRA to Policy: The Conflict Analysis Framework. *PLA Notes* 27, *Participation, Policy and Institutionalisation*, International Institute for Environment and Development, London.